Golf Courses

A Guide to Analysis and Valuation

GOLF COURSES
A Guide to Analysis and Valuation

Prepared in Collaboration with Cecil McKay, Jr.

by

Karla L. Heuer, AIREA Publications Editor

Published by the
American Institute of Real Estate Appraisers
430 North Michigan Avenue • Chicago, Illinois

For Educational Purposes Only

The opinions and statements set forth herein are those of the individual contributors or the individual members of the Institute's editorial staff and do not necessarily reflect the viewpoint of the American Institute of Real Estate Appraisers or its individual members.

Copyright © by the American Institute of Real Estate Appraisers of the National Association of Realtors, an Illinois Not For Profit Corporation, 1980. All rights reserved.

ISBN: 0-911780-47-5
Printed in the United States of America

Foreword

Although general appraisal processes have been developed and are applicable to just about any property type, the unique elements of any special purpose property require additional insight on the part of the appraiser or analyst. This is the reason the American Institute of Real Estate Appraisers offers information on special purpose properties through its series of research monographs. *Golf Courses: A Guide to Analysis and Valuation* provides the appraiser and other property consultants a detailed look at the developmental, operational, and financial aspects that are essential factors in the analysis of a golf course. It should serve as a companion volume to earlier Institute monographs on hotels and motels, tennis clubs, condominiums, shopping centers, and roadway signs.

> John R. Remick, MAI
> 1979 President
> American Institute of Real Estate Appraisers

Acknowledgments

Like an appraisal report, this monograph presents data gathered from a variety of sources, including organizations and individuals whose knowledge about the design, development, and operation of golf courses was invaluable.

Foremost recognition goes to Cecil McKay, Jr., of McKay Golf and Country Club Properties, Lansing, Michigan. One of few golf course brokers in the United States, Mr. McKay has "walked" courses throughout the country. He shared his data and personal knowledge, and without his cooperation and assistance, the monograph would not be possible in its present format.

Acknowledgment and thanks go to Edward B. Atherton, MAI, of Fairfax, Virginia, whose contribution was the base for the discussion of highest and best use in relation to golf courses.

The Institute also wishes to thank the following organizations and individuals for their input: the Urban Land Institute; Gerald F. Hurley of the National Club Association; Don Rossi of the National Golf Foundation; and Carl Swartskopf of the United States Golf Association, Greens Section. Data was also provided by golf course architects Gerald Matthews, Lansburg, Michigan; Hassenplug Associates, Inc., Pittsburgh, Pennsylvania; Thomson Wolveridge Fream & Associates, Los Gatos, California; as well as the Johns-Manville Corp.; the Rainbird Irrigation Company; and Jim Bogart of O. M. Scotts Company.

Arlington Lakes Golf Club, Arlington Heights, Illinois, was used as an example in several sections of the monograph. Larry Maholland, of the

Arlington Heights Park District, was most helpful, as was the course's architect, David Gill of the David Gill Corp., St. Charles, Illinois. Mr. Gill not only supplied data but also served as a reviewer of the final manuscript.

Thanks are also extended to the Institute's review committee: Robert W. Dombal, MAI, Chairman of the Publications Committee; Jerome N. Block, MAI; James C. Kafes, MAI; and Peter D. Bowes, MAI.

The illustrations on pages x, 2, 8, 18, 20, 26, 36, 56, 100, and 110 are reprinted with permission through the courtesy of International Golf Promotions, Inc., Elk Grove Village, Illinois.

Contents

	Foreword	v
	Acknowledgments	vii
1	Introduction	1
2	Market Analysis	9
3	Development	19
4	Site Analysis and Valuation	27
5	Golf Course Improvements	37
6	Golf Course Operations	57
7	Valuation Procedures	101
8	Valuation Under Eminent Domain	111
	Appendix	115
	Selected Bibliography	125
	Sources for Information	127

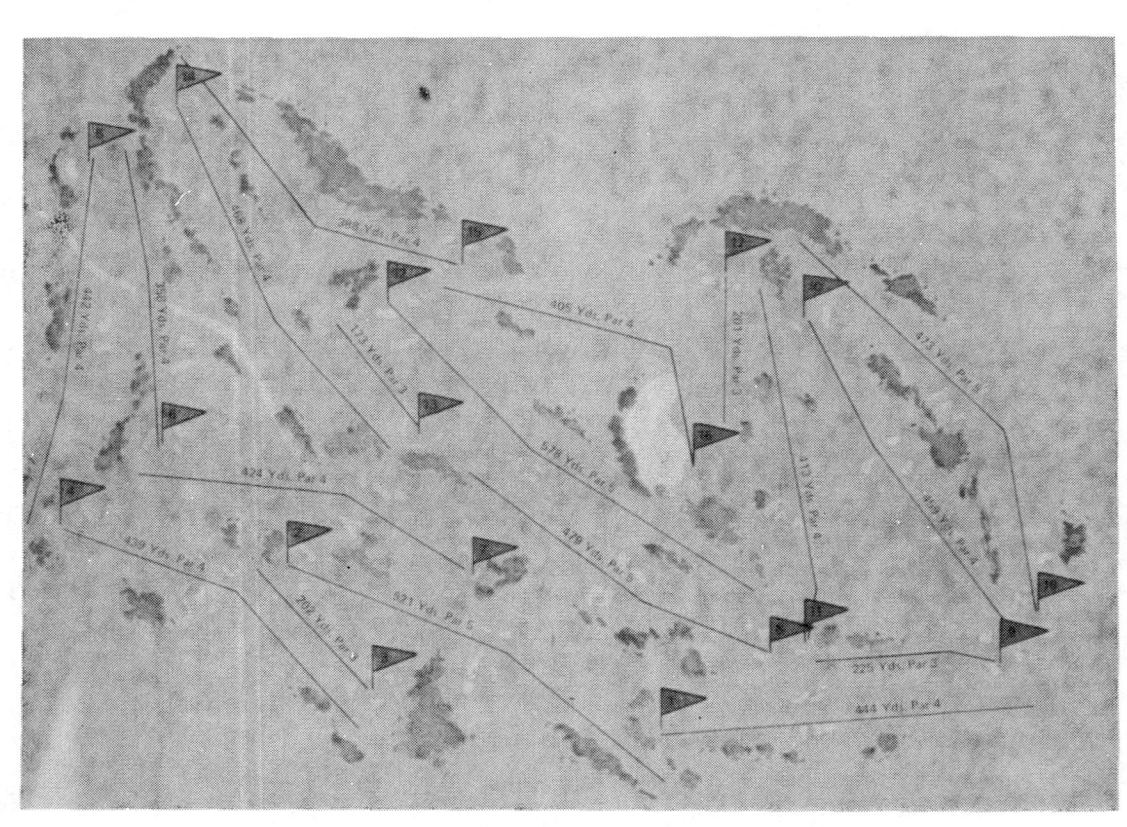

1

Introduction

Although its name is derived from the Dutch word *kolf* (club), the game of golf as played in the United States originated in Scotland during the 15th century. Attesting to its popularity is the decree issued by the 14th parliament of King James II that "golfe be utterly cryed down, and not to be used" because avid players were neglecting archery, which was necessary for defense. Subsequent bans were equally ineffective, and the game finally gained acceptance among the royalty, providing them the chance to relax and enjoy nature.[1]

St. Andrews, Scotland, is said to be the birthplace of golf; and Mary, Queen of Scots, played there in the mid-16th century. A completely natural linksland course along the seashore, it was the first formal golf course. The Royal and Ancient Golf Club of St. Andrews, formed on May 14, 1754, became the determinant authority on game rules, which were the basis for shaping golf in the United States.

An advertisement in James Rivington's *Gazette* in New York in April 1779 is the first recorded mention of golf in the United States: "To the Golf Players: The season for this pleasant and healthy exercise now advancing,

---

1. "Golf," in *Encyclopaedia Britannica,* Vol. 10 (Chicago: Encyclopaedia Britannica, Inc., 1970), p. 549.

Golf courses in the U.S. represent a capital investment of $4.8 billion in almost 1,300,000 acres of land.

gentlemen may be furnished with excellent clubs and veritable Caledonian balls by enquiring at the Printer's."[2]

The first permanent golf club and course in the United States was established in 1887 at Foxburg, Pennsylvania. A club formed the next year, the St. Andrews Golf Club of Yonkers, New York, was instrumental in organizing the first golf association. With its purpose being to establish uniform rules and to conduct tournaments, the Amateur Golf Association of the United States was created on December 22, 1894. Eventually named the United States Golf Association, it was soon followed by the Western Golf Association in 1899 and the Professional Golfers Association of America in 1916.

From these beginnings, golf in the United States has grown to include about 15,855,000 players who play an estimated 336,600,000 rounds a year. More than 12.6 million of them play 15 or more rounds a year. An estimated 1,273,000 acres of land are devoted to golf courses. With course improvements, this represents a capital investment of $4.8 billion; annual expenditure for maintenance is approximately $778,000,000.[3]

Golf course development peaked in the late 1960s when an average of about 400 courses a year were built throughout the country, largely by developers of vast real estate projects. The golf course was included as a sales amenity, and design was often geared toward maximum lot frontage. Falling to a low of 190 new golf facilities in 1976, development is beginning to pick up; 1977 saw a 7% gain in new courses and additions. Increased leisure time, heightened interest in the game because of televised matches, and expected personal rewards from participation are some of the reasons given for growth of the game. In addition, the outlook for golf as part of real estate developments is promising. The energy crisis emphasizes the logic of living, working, and playing in one environment.

These 1979 National Golf Foundation statistics demonstrate the steady growth of facilities.[4]

Number of Facilities

1950	4,931
1960	6,385
1970	10,188
1978	11,885

---

2. *Ibid.*, p. 550
3. Statistics throughout this chapter are from *Golf Facilities in the United States* (North Palm Beach, FL: National Golf Foundation, 1979).
4. The term *facility* is used for a single geographical area that contains one or more golf courses under one management.

Golf courses can be tremendous community assets. They provide healthy and enjoyable recreation, raise property values in surrounding areas, attract industry, stimulate civic pride, and create new business. Although municipal facilities account for only 14.7% of the total number of courses, 38.8% of the golfers in America use these facilities, and many more public courses could be used.

TYPES OF GOLF COURSES

The two types of golf courses, classified by size, are the regulation-sized course and the short course.

Regulation-sized courses may be either 9-hole (about 3,200 yards long with a par 35 rating) or 18-hole (about 6,500 yards long with a standard par 72 rating). Some 9-hole courses have two sets of tees which vary the length, and each hole is played twice for an 18-hole round. A regulation-sized course is designed according to one of five basic configurations:

1. Single fairway 18-hole course with returning nines
2. Single fairway continuous 18-hole course
3. Double fairway 18-hole course with returning nines
4. Double fairway continuous 18-hole course
5. Core course

Land requirements for the various configurations vary. Minimum acreage is 110 acres, with a range for an ideal course from about 140 acres to about 175 acres. A single fairway 18-hole course with returning nines or a single fairway continuous 18-hole course should be about 175 acres. A double fairway 18-hole course with returning nines or a double fairway continuous 18-hole course should be about 150 acres. The core course, designed for compactness, can be built on 110 acres, but a 140-acre site is preferable. See Figure 1.1 for an illustration of the configurations.

A combination of the basic configurations may also be used to accommodate requirements of users or site characteristics and topography.

Short courses gained popularity after World War II when the number of players burgeoned; they appeal to golfers whose time and energy is limited. The advantages of short courses include smaller land area; lower construction, operating, and maintenance costs; and shorter playing time. There are three kinds of short courses:

Figure 1.1. Configuration of Regulation Golf Courses.

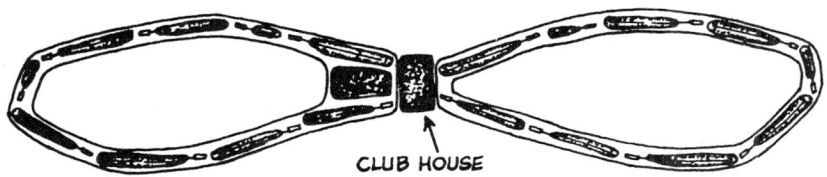

1. SINGLE FAIRWAY 18-HOLE COURSE WITH RETURNING NINES

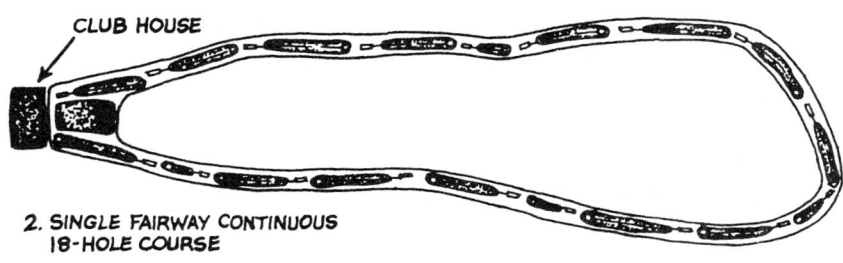

2. SINGLE FAIRWAY CONTINUOUS 18-HOLE COURSE

3. DOUBLE FAIRWAY 18-HOLE COURSE WITH RETURNING NINES

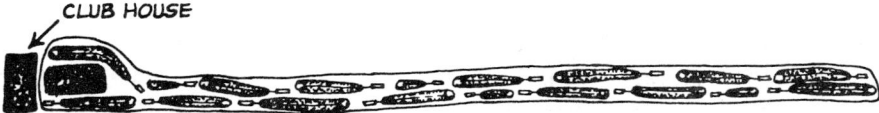

4. DOUBLE FAIRWAY CONTINUOUS 18-HOLE COURSE

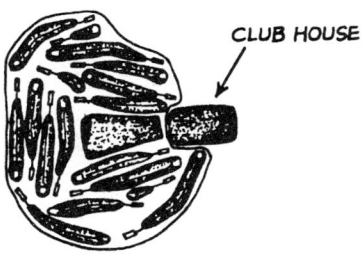

5. CORE GOLF COURSE

Reprinted with permission from *Golf Course Development,* Technical Bulletin 70 (Washington, DC: Urban Land Institute, 1974).

1. Pitch and putt
2. Par 3
3. Executive

Pitch and putt courses can be built on as little as 10 acres. Holes are generally less than 100 yards and can be played with a pitching iron and putter. Par 3 courses can be either 9 holes or 18 holes. Holes are all par 3, with a maximum yardage of 250. They are built on 20 to 35 acres with the length being 500 to 1,400 yards. An average player can play a par 3 course in 45 minutes to an hour. Executive courses are par 55 to 67, with some holes that are more than par 3. They require 50 to 100 acres of land.

PRIVATE, DAILY-FEE, AND MUNICIPAL COURSES

A major problem in estimating the value of a golf course is defining the operational category of the course being appraised. It may be one of three kinds:

1. Private
2. Daily-fee
3. Municipal

Within each of these categories is a wide range of situations.

Private courses are primarily thought of as member-owned, exclusive, and nonprofit. In reality, many private clubs are now owned by individuals and are operated as profit-making entities. Sometimes the club itself is nonprofit, but all club facilities are leased to a profit-making entity.

Municipal courses are owned by tax-supported government bodies that, in the past, have operated them as recreational facilities for the people of the community. As the golf industry is rapidly changing from a private, nonprofit kind of business, a new trend is to lease municipal golf courses to concessionaires who operate them for profit.

By far the largest growth in golf facilities has been daily-fee courses. From 1955 to 1975, the total increase for all types of courses was 118%, but for daily fee courses it was 227%. These operations, which are open to the public, are owned by individuals, partnerships, or corporations as businesses. Although daily-fee courses may offer member privileges, they are open to public patrons who pay a fee to play.

In 1978 there were more than 11,885 golf facilities in the United States. Of these, 41% were private, 14.6% were municipal, and 44.4% were daily fee. Table 1.1 shows their distribution among regulation-sized and short courses.

Table 1.1 Number of Regulation-Sized and Short Courses

	9-hole	18-hole	Total
Regulation courses			
Private	1,907	2,945	4,852
Daily fee	2,221	2,259	4,480
Municipal	635	1,007	1,642
	4,763	6,211	10,974
Executive courses			
Private	86	31	117
Daily fee	299	180	479
Municipal	17	25	96
	456	236	692
Par-3 courses			
Private	168	31	199
Daily fee	478	185	663
Municipal	120	36	156
	766	252	1,018
Total	5,985	6,699	12,684

Source: *Golf Facilities in the United States* (North Palm Beach, FL: National Golf Foundation, 1979).

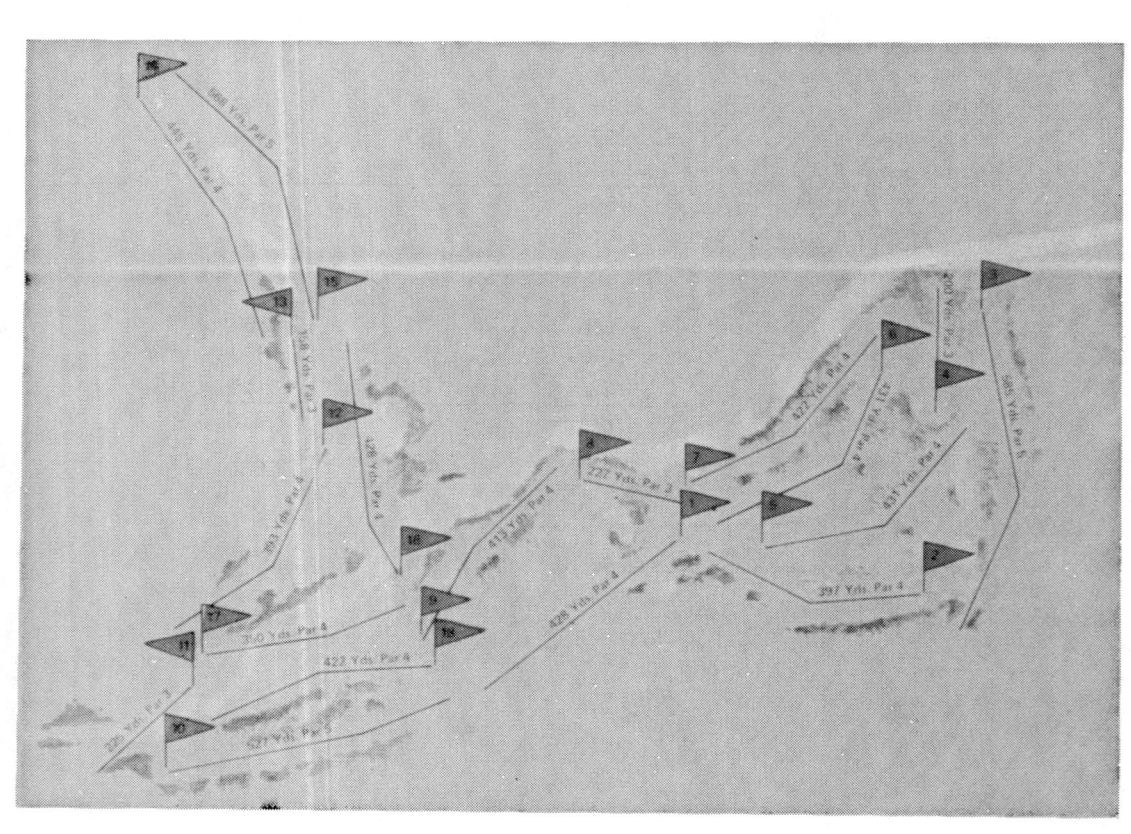

2

Market Analysis

In all appraisal assignments the compilation and analysis of regional and local data are important. In the appraisal of a golf course this kind of data is particularly essential. The appraiser must be cognizant of supply and demand factors in the neighborhood from which the golf course will draw members or patrons.

The neighborhood may be delineated as part of a community, an entire community, or a large region. The appraiser should keep in mind that avid golfers will travel a long distance to play a particularly good course and will avoid a bad course even if it is close by. Therefore, determining the trade area is a prerequisite to a study of supply and demand factors, which weigh heavily in the market value of a golf course.

An additional factor in the necessary feasibility analysis is economic. Demand is effective only when people are financially able to satisfy their desires. Therefore, the appraiser must also consider the makeup of the population that will support the golf course. Among the factors to be considered are:

1. Population
2. Growth rates
3. Age statistics
4. Income levels
5. Recreatronal preferences

BENEFITS OF A GOLF COURSE

An obvious benefit of a golf course is as a recreational facility. But there are also intangible advantages in its open space, tranquility, and aesthetic value. In a well-designed course the principles of art—harmony, proportion, balance, rhythm, and emphasis—are present. A golf course can be an ecological asset. It can be a haven for birds and other small wildlife, and it produces fresh air as turf and trees take in carbon dioxide and various pollutants and give off oxygen.

A golf course enhances the image of a community; and as part of a development, it offers a great public relations tool. It can improve a developer's ability to obtain the necessary zoning approvals or at least to operate more flexibly within zoning requirements. In a dense cluster plan a developer may obtain zoning approval upon the promise that a considerable amount of open space will be included in the project. A park would satisfy the requirement, but a golf course will sell homes. In some instances developers build a golf course and eventually turn it over to the municipality. The developer realizes an increase in real estate value; the local government assumes maintenance expenses; and the community has a recreational facility.

Residential home sites along a golf course are prestige addresses, and the value of these sites experiences an accelerated rate of appreciation that is more than is attributable to normal inflationary factors. A lot along a fairway may sell for as much as $10,000 more than a similar lot elsewhere.[1]

A golf course that is part of a development is an inducement to buyers. Almost half the new courses that are being built today are part of larger real estate developments. In a development of higher-priced homes, a golf course provides an instant prestige atmosphere and may even be thought of as a necessity. People who are not golfers also like the atmosphere and may buy in a development with a golf course because of the parklike setting. It brings potential buyers from a wider area than might otherwise be considered the market area.

In retirement, adult, and second home resort areas, a golf course may be an expected amenity. It also diversifies the types and increases the number of land uses for surrounding properties. Golf villas, cottages, and/or a motel become possibilities.

A developer who is presenting a project for financing may be at an advantage if a golf course is included in the plans. Because it is different

---

1. *Rising Property Taxes—Can Anything Be Done?* National Club Association Reference Series (Washington, DC: National Club Association, 1976), p. 4.

from the typical or competing development, it may be viewed more favorably by financial sources.

Finally, a golf course can be a profit-making venture. The key to financial success for a new course is careful planning and, as for all courses, good maintenance and management.

The benefits of a golf course vary from community to community. What will be seen as a benefit in one locale may not be in another. Benefits must be viewed as they relate to the specific location of the subject golf course.

DEMAND

Extensive research is necessary to ascertain the demand for golfing facilities in an area. A long-standing general estimate of the number of people necessary to support a golf course is 20,000 to 30,000 people per 18-hole course, with an additional 18-hole course for each 30,000 people. Because of more leisure time, more disposable income, and the heightened popularity of the game, however, more recent indications are that a population of 10,000 can support a course in an area where golf is a favored recreation. In resort or retirement communities a golf course may be warranted for a population as small as 2,500 to 5,000 if there are enough ardent golfers in the population.

An example of divergence from the "rule-of-thumb" population-to-course estimate is Grand Rapids, Michigan, which has more golf courses per population and more rounds played per course than any other community in the state. Grand Rapids is simply a community in which there is a high interest in the game. A converse example is a town of 25,000 in Arkansas which has one golf course. Although this would seem to be an ideal situation, the golf course is not heavily used because there is little interest in golf in the community. A variety of golfing facilities is necessary to build up patronage for the game in a community.

Statistics, such as those published by the National Golf Foundation, of estimated rounds of golf by geographic division, are a helpful starting point for the appraiser in assessing demand. However, a professional market analysis must be conducted locally. Although the appraiser may know that almost 16 million golfers across the country play more than 300 million rounds a year, what is salient is how many golfers play how many rounds of golf in the community in which the golf course being appraised is located.

Composition of the Community

Demand is affected by the nature of the community. Data the appraiser gathers will include specifics about the type of people living in the area; whether the community is growing, static, or declining; the ages of the population; the type of community (i.e., agricultural, industrial, or residential); the income level of the residents; the recreational preferences of the population, how far they will travel for recreation, and what they will be willing to pay for it. Influences within the community—for example, attitudes toward a golf course operating on Sunday or the sale of beer and liquor—affect the income of a golf course and hence its market value.

Income Factors

The appraiser will need to know the per capita income of the area and if it is running parallel to regional and national trends. Whether the golf course being appraised is private, daily fee, or municipal will be considered by the appraiser in determining patronage from among community residents. Members of a private country club will need sufficient income to afford the dues, fees, and similar assessments that support the club. Membership in a daily fee course is generally less expensive, and the members' incomes will probably reflect this. The appraiser will also relate the cost of play at a daily fee course or a municipal course to the income of area residents.

Employment patterns in the area affect the income of a golf course. For example, a golf course that depends in large part upon players who are factory workers working many overtime hours will suffer. Although the potential golfers have more money to spend, they have no time to play golf. However, during a layoff, play at area golf courses increases. Golfers may not buy expensive equipment at this time, but the need for activity will bring them out to the golf course. Trips to vacation areas may be put off, which increases the business of local golf courses.

The connotation of golf as purely "a rich man's pursuit" is not necessarily true. In fact, most golfers at daily fee clubs are blue-collar workers. The cost of playing golf is less per hour than many other sports (e.g., bowling, boating, skiing), and the cost of equipment is also less.

The effect between income and the cost of play can be analyzed on the basis of type of player. One study[2] of the demand for golfing services divided

---

2. Robert Louis Milam, "An Analysis of the Demand for Selected Golfing Services in the North Carolina Piedmont," *The Appraisal Journal* (October 1970), p. 608.

players into five categories: 1) all players, 2) weekend patrons, 3) weekday patrons, 4) members, and 5) nonmembers.

The results of this study by Robert Milam showed that the net effect between income and cost to play was positive for weekday patrons, nonmembers, and all patrons. For each of these types of players, the effect of income on number of rounds per year was highly significant. For weekend patrons and members, it was not significant. From these and other results, the study inferred that cost is generally a consideration for golfers.

The Milam study also points out that a distinguishing characteristic of golf is that the consumer must provide an economic good (time) during the process of using the course. Hence in a study of demand for golfing facilities, unlike a conventional demand study, the price of time to an individual playing golf is a significant factor.

Age

Age is not the factor that it would be in a market study for tennis, for example, because golf is a game that can be played across a wide age span. However, in a community with many young children, the families are more likely to put their recreational dollars into membership at a swimming pool, which the children can enjoy, than into a golf club membership, which would be used primarily by the parents.

Climate

The market analysis includes study of the regional climate and weather patterns, including items such as wind direction and velocity and the frequency of storms that would make playing golf impossible.

The estimated number of rounds of play for golf courses is directly related to climate and the length of the season of the region in which the course is located. In the South a maximum number of rounds might be 90,000; in the middle states, 60,000; and in the northern states, 40,000. A course in Florida or Southern California with year-round operation may seem more attractive for investors or developers, but courses in the northern United States can also be profitable. Because the playing season is only seven or eight months long, the majority of expenses are also limited to seven or eight months, so that during the off season, expenditures are minimized. Southern courses also have an off season, but their expenses continue throughout the year. That northern courses are capable of producing good strong golf income is demonstrated in Table 2.1.

Table 2.1. The Case for the Northern Course

	Location				
	Michigan	N.E. Ohio	Minnesota	S.E. Florida	Central Georgia
Asking price	$1,300,000	$1,300,000	$1,300,000	$2,500,000*	$ 900,000
Income source					
Green fees	$237,188	$179,759	$151,992	$158,340	$ 42,831
Memberships	—	3,727	18,277	33,197	112,058
Golf cart rentals	42,451	26,547	33,217	265,062	30,447
Range rentals and other	13,120	3,064	11,398	30,500	30,022
Restaurant	92,137	53 632	61,161	94,735	
Bar	71,288			76,864	111,682
Pro shop	20,882	95,756	26,102	67,221	
Total sales	$477,066	$362,485	$302,147	$725,919	$327,040

* This course is in a densely populated area, hence the price is higher than any of the other selected courses.

These figures are not indicative of the peak income courses can produce, but they are in line with what can be expected in the area.

Severe weather conditions for a single year can have an adverse effect on the entire golf industry. For example, the NGF reported that the bad winter and spring of 1978 caused a slowdown of facility development, player development, and the amount of golf play throughout the nation. The bad weather in New England in 1977 caused a 30% decrease in play in that area. The appraiser will study the effects of weather on golf in a region over several years.

Trade Area

A golf course is immobile and must draw consumers to it by a combination of intangibles, such as the feeling of well being the golfer experiences from time spent on the course, and tangibles such as the quality and challenge of the course. A quality course is planned for the game of golf itself, eye appeal, and future maintenance. The appraiser will have to judge the quality of a course in determining the trade area and thus the income potential of the course. One of the best sources for an opinion of the quality of a course is the golfers who play the course.

Golf course architects and builders may argue the question of whether a course should cater to low- or high-handicap players, short or long hitters, and championship or regular play. In fact, a course can be designed to be played by all kinds of players. Strategic design can make a course challenging for the excellent golfer, but not too difficult for the less skilled player. Such a course is not so easy that it is uninteresting or so difficult that it is frustrating, and it appeals to players of varying skill. It is likely to attract golfers from a wider area than the ordinary course.

In fixing the trade area, the appraiser should also explore plans for new developments in the community: new highways, subdivisions, industry, and other factors that may influence the growth of the community and hence the potential for an increased number of patrons for the golf course being appraised. Local planning commissions are the best source for this data. Growth patterns in the area can be obtained from the state's Department of Conservation and Economic Development.

SUPPLY

A study of the supply of golf courses to meet the demand is the final phase of the market analysis. The appraiser researches the number of private, daily fee, and municipal golf courses and relates this to the demand that has been determined for the area.

Simply because there are enough courses to meet the population-per-course criterion does not mean that the supply is commensurate to the demand. Courses may not be attracting members or patrons because of poor management or inadequate maintenance. A course may be designed for only the most skilled golfers or be so uninteresting that it does not encourage repeat play. A course may be inaccessible due to poor roads leading to it. There may be enough municipal courses, but the population may desire the amenities of a private club. A development may have a golf course that is not open to the public, overburdening a municipal course. A private country club may be too expensive for the general income level of the community. Plans may be in process for a new course that would cut into the business of existing courses.

Figure 2.1. Community Golf Profile Report

No._____

WORKSHEET

CITY _____ COUNTY _____ STATE _____

POPULATION: CITY SMSA

    1950 _____ _____
    1960 _____ _____
    1970 _____ _____
    1977 _____ _____
    1980 Projected _____ _____

MEDIAN FAMILY INCOME—1977: CITY _____ SMSA _____

CLIMATE: AVERAGE TEMPERATURE: January _____ April _____ July _____ October _____
               AVERAGE LENGTH OF GOLF SEASON: _____ Days

NUMBER OF   PUBLIC COURSES: 9 HOLE   18 HOLE
                DAILY FEE _____ _____
                MUNICIPAL _____ _____

PLEASE ATTACH LIST OF PUBLIC COURSES (include name, type, number of holes and comments)

NUMBER OF PRIVATE COURSES _____
OTHER TYPES (Industrial, military, etc.) _____
ESTIMATED GOLFERS IN SMSA: MEN _____ WOMEN _____
ESTIMATED ROUNDS PLAYED IN SMSA _____
STATE OF GOLF INSTRUCTION (Describe instructional programs, availability of practice facilities, etc.)

AT COURSES

_____
_____
_____

KEY PERSONNEL (with address)

_____
_____

AGENCIES (Parks & Recreation Departments, etc.)

_____
_____

KEY PERSONNEL (with address)

_____
_____

SCHOOL DISTRICTS, COLLEGES, COMMUNITY COLLEGES, ETC.

_____
_____

KEY PERSONNEL (with address)

_____
_____

ADDITIONAL COMMENTS: _____

_____
_____

What this all means is that the appraiser must study the local demand and relate it to the local supply. No player-per-course generalization will do. Personal observation and judgment are required. As well as using the usual demographic reporting sources, the appraiser should talk to people in the area who are involved in golf to determine the amount of interest in the game and the quality of the facilities and if they are meeting the demand.

In 1978 the NGF developed a plan for a comprehensive canvas of each major area of the country to determine the state of golf in the area. Concentration is currently being directed toward developing a profile of every city of 50,000 or larger population. This information is filed at the NGF headquarters.

A standard Community Golf Profile Report is used by the NGF (see Figure 2.1). It provides information such as 1) city and market populations; 2) past, present, and projected growth rates; 3) brief description of area characteristics; 4) weather conditions as they affect golf; 5) summary of player development programs; 6) list of public golf facilities available; and 7) roster of key individuals in the community in golf operations, development, and instruction. This is the kind of information the appraiser needs as part of a market analysis in appraising a golf course. The emphasis must be local.

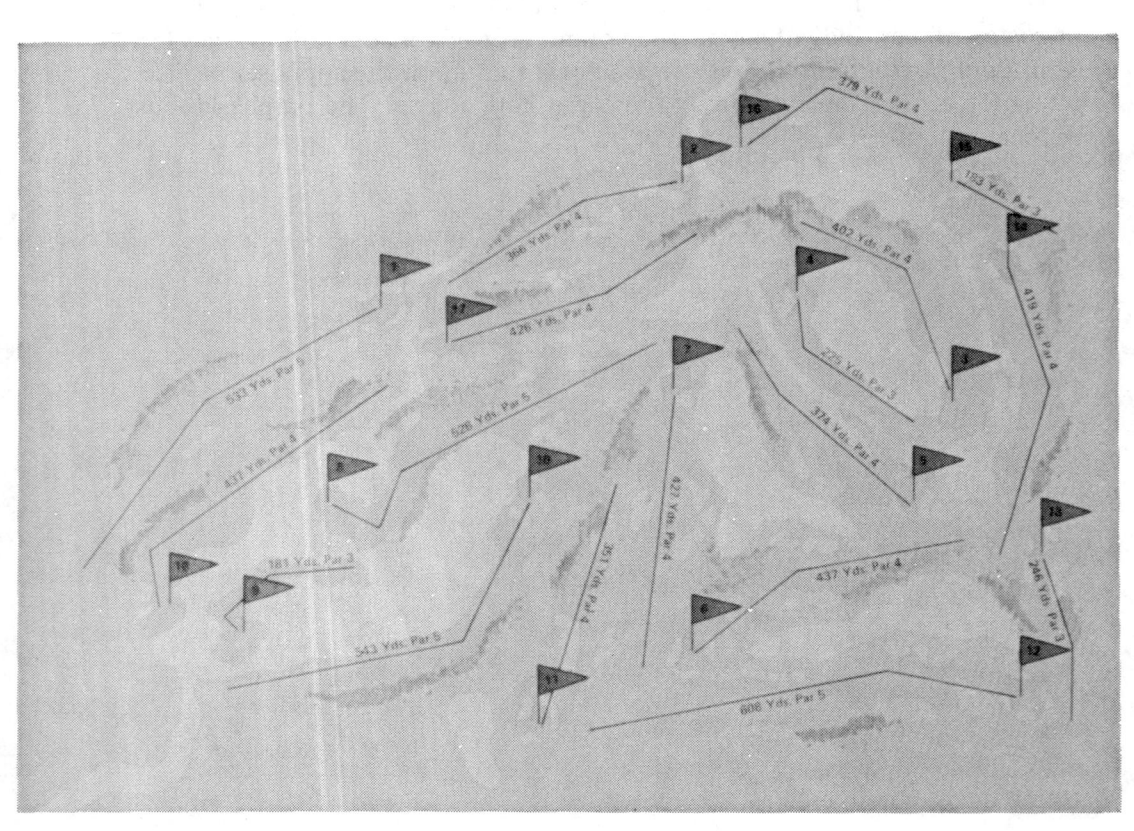

3

Development

Designing and building a golf course is an exercise in problem solving. An awareness of the complexities involved is a prerequisite to planning. Before any work begins, the developer should provide for:

1. A competent golf course architect
2. Site selection
3. Plans and specifications
4. Financing
5. Construction
6. Maintenance and supervision

ARCHITECT

Creative design, knowledgeable construction, and proper turfgrass maintenance are the keys to the success of a golf course. A qualified professional golf course architect is an expert in these areas. It is important to have a clear understanding with the architect from the beginning of the project as to exactly what kind of course is needed. For example, a development of luxury homes can support a more expensive course than a development of mid-priced homes.

The golf course architect is particularly helpful at the time that acreage

Gently rolling terrain with the proper soil is desirable for a golf course site.

for the course is being decided upon since the decision is based on width and length of fairways; distance from previous green to the next tee; the extent of roughs, trees, lakes, and wasted triangles between holes; and the topography and condition of the land. Natural features of the site will be incorporated into the design, as the architect keeps in mind knowledge of soil, horticulture, and golf course construction. Future maintenance is a primary concern at this point since excessive maintenance costs can usually be related to weaknesses in the original design.

A knowledge of total land planning is required if the golf course is to be part of a residential development. The architect will help in delineating specific areas for golf and for adjacent land use and will plan for enhancing real estate.

Laying out the golf course and supervising construction are the primary responsibilities of the golf course architect. Plans may look good on the drawing board, but there is no substitute for on-the-ground study and regular visits of inspection as construction proceeds.

The reputation of an experienced golf course architect can be checked with the owners of courses previously designed by the architect. Membership in the American Society of Golf Course Architects also is an indication of professional standing.

SITE SELECTION

A gently rolling area with some trees and natural features to make the game interesting may appear to be the perfect golf course site. But many factors must be considered before a choice is made. Suitable soil, preferably sandy loam, is of utmost importance, and it should be in good condition. On a rundown farm, for example, most of the soil's natural plant food may be depleted, and excessive amounts of fertilizer will be needed for proper cultivation of the turf. Well-maintained pastureland usually makes a good golf course site. Special geographic conditions, such as rocky soils, high alkaline content of the soil, high winds, and salt sprays, must also be considered when selecting the site.

Although floodplain land and land fills may be utilized for golf courses, their particular problems must be evaluated. A golf course built on a floodplain may have a lower economic value than one built in a high and dry area because of the hazards of flooding, possible interruption of play, and cleanup costs. A relatively new idea is to build a golf course on a land fill. However, shifting and settling of the land, the release of methane gas from deteriorating rubbish, and other special maintenance problems must be considered.

The suggested minimum size for a 9-hole course is 50 acres for level terrain and 70 to 90 acres for a hilly site. An 18-hole course requires at least 110 acres; but if the terrain is rough, 140 to 175 acres may be necessary.

Other factors to be considered in selecting the site are: location, accessibility, zoning, size and shape of site, topography, soil, drainage, vegetation, water, and utilities. These considerations are discussed in Chapter 4.

PLANS AND SPECIFICATIONS

The golf course architect will prepare plans and specifications. General specifications as well as details for grading, planting, and irrigation make up the full set of plans. Included in these categories are subsurface drainage; correct, scientifically analyzed seedbed mixtures for putting greens and tee areas; and environmentally adapted turfgrass varieties.

Because surface features are secondary to what is under the surface, a golf course architect with expertise in playing conditions and turfgrass culture can benefit the developer. Unless future problems are anticipated, they will mushroom and assure failure for the operation. The decision at this point to use quality methods and materials will prevent costly future problems.

Because the irrigation system can be the most costly and problematic element of the project, it should be designed by a professional engineer who specializes in irrigation systems.

FINANCING

Private investors, insurance companies, and the Small Business Administration are possible sources of financing for a golf course. Especially if the course is part of a larger real estate development project, arrangements can be made with banks and savings and loans. Local governments can sell general obligation or revenue bonds or work out an arrangement with a private developer to build the course and lease it back to the municipality.

Several federal aid programs are available to municipalities. The most popular is the 50% matching grant plan of the HCRC (Heritage Conservation and Recreations Services, formerly the Bureau of Outdoor Recreation) of the Department of the Interior. The program provides matching grants to states and through states to their political subdivisions for the acquisition and development of public outdoor recreation areas and facilities.

Since the program was authorized in 1965, $1.7 billion in matching grants have been made to purchase over 1.9 million acres of land and to fund development of recreational facilities. For 1978, over $306 million was approved nationwide for this program. Apportionments to the 50 states ranged from approximately $21 million for California to about $2 million for Wyoming. Many municipalities throughout the nation have developed or acquired existing golf courses with the aid of matching grants.

Other possible federal assistance programs include the Surplus Property Program, administered by the HCRC; the Federal Revenue Sharing Program, administered by the Office of Revenue Sharing, U.S. Treasury Department, and implemented by municipalities; and the Department of Housing and Urban Development Community Development Funds, which are administered by the 10 area offices of HUD.[1]

CONSTRUCTION

The bases for selecting a contractor are experience, demonstrated ability, willingness to adhere strictly to contract terms, and fee. Contracts will include established prices, completion schedules, bonus and penalty clauses, provisions for inspections, contingencies, and dismissal for nonperformance.

A fully experienced golf course superintendent on the site during construction is a valuable asset. Directing the day-to-day construction process, the superintendent can interpret plans and specifications for the contractor. The golf course architect should also visit the site regularly. However, the only changes during construction should be minor modifications or stylistic adjustments.

Costs for daily fee golf courses typically range between $17,000 and $25,000 per hole, depending on terrain, climate, labor, water supply, and type of course.[2] Private golf courses may cost as much as $1.5 million ($83,000+ per hole) because the primary consideration is providing exactly what the membership wants and is willing to pay for.

Course construction can take from 10 months to two years, depending on complexity and weather patterns.

---

1. Harry C. Eckhoff, "Guidelines for Planning and Building a Golf Course," *Public Works* (July 1978).
2. "Investing in Golf Courses," *Real Estate Investing Letter* (January 1979), p. 2.

MAINTENANCE

A well-designed golf course is one for which maintenance costs can be kept to a minimum. Suggestions for design features that will help to reduce maintenance include:

1. Make all grades mowable by a 9-gang hydraulic lift fairway mower. Make certain that there are no lumps or hollows that need handwork. Try to keep all grades 10% or less. Design the course to accommodate 3-, 5-, and 7-unit mowers in areas too tight for a full gang mower. If possible, keep all the maintenance personnel in vehicles of some kind. The use of new triplex greens mowers is increasing, so make sure there is room on the green collar for them to turn.
2. Keep trees grouped and at least 12 to 15 feet apart to facilitate mowing. Pines and other softwoods are a good selection because they are usually easy to maintain. Some evergreens and fin-leafed hardwoods are also easy to care for. Avoid large numbers of broad-leafed hardwoods that will need daily sweeping.
3. Keep size of greens reasonable. For instance, 12,000-square-foot greens may require two or more extra people per course above the number needed if the course had 7,000-square-foot greens. Greens should have 70 to 85% of the area available for pin placement.[3]

Although many experts advise that a fully automatic irrigation system is essential to reduce maintenance costs, others suggest that the economics involved may preclude this expense. An automatic system gives more uniform coverage than a manual system, but it is not necessarily economically advantageous. Fully automatic systems are more common at private clubs than at daily fee courses. The latter usually have pop-up heads around the greens and perhaps the tees, but the fairways are watered manually. The price of a fully automatic system may be $50,000 to $100,000 more than a manual system. This may not be economically feasible for a profit-oriented golf course. Labor costs to have the course watered manually may be less than the cost of an automatic system. In addition, a person who can operate

---

3. Desmond Muirhead, "Building the Golf Course," in *Land: Recreation & Leisure* (Washington, DC: Urban Land Institute, 1970), pp. 25-26.

an automatic system must understand the intricacies of the system and how to program it, for which the person will command a higher salary.

Planning for low maintenance costs is particularly necessary in view of the fact that these costs have virtually tripled over the past 10 years. Statistics from the national accounting firm of Harris, Kerr, Forster & Company for 1978 show that for 100 private clubs with a total of 2,070 holes of golf, maintenance costs were 7.6% greater than the year before, and net golf expenses showed an overall advance of 8.4%. The upward trend was evident for private clubs in all of the geographical divisions. In maintenance costs per hole for five-year periods, Harris, Kerr, Forster figures show that from 1958 to 1963 costs increased 19.8%; from 1963 to 1968, 26.3%; from 1968 to 1973, 36.9%; and from 1973 to 1978, 45.5%.[4]

A good investment of maintenance funds is for a superior golf course superintendent. Estimates as high as 25% of the maintenance budget have been suggested for a high-caliber person, but a customary annual salary ranges from $12,000 to $25,000. An experienced supervisor, educated in turfgrass maintenance, can assure that even a mediocre course is maintained at a level that makes it better for play than a great course that is not so well maintained.

---

4. *Clubs in Town & Country 1978* (New York: Harris, Kerr, Forster & Company, Certified Public Accountants, 1979), p. 17.

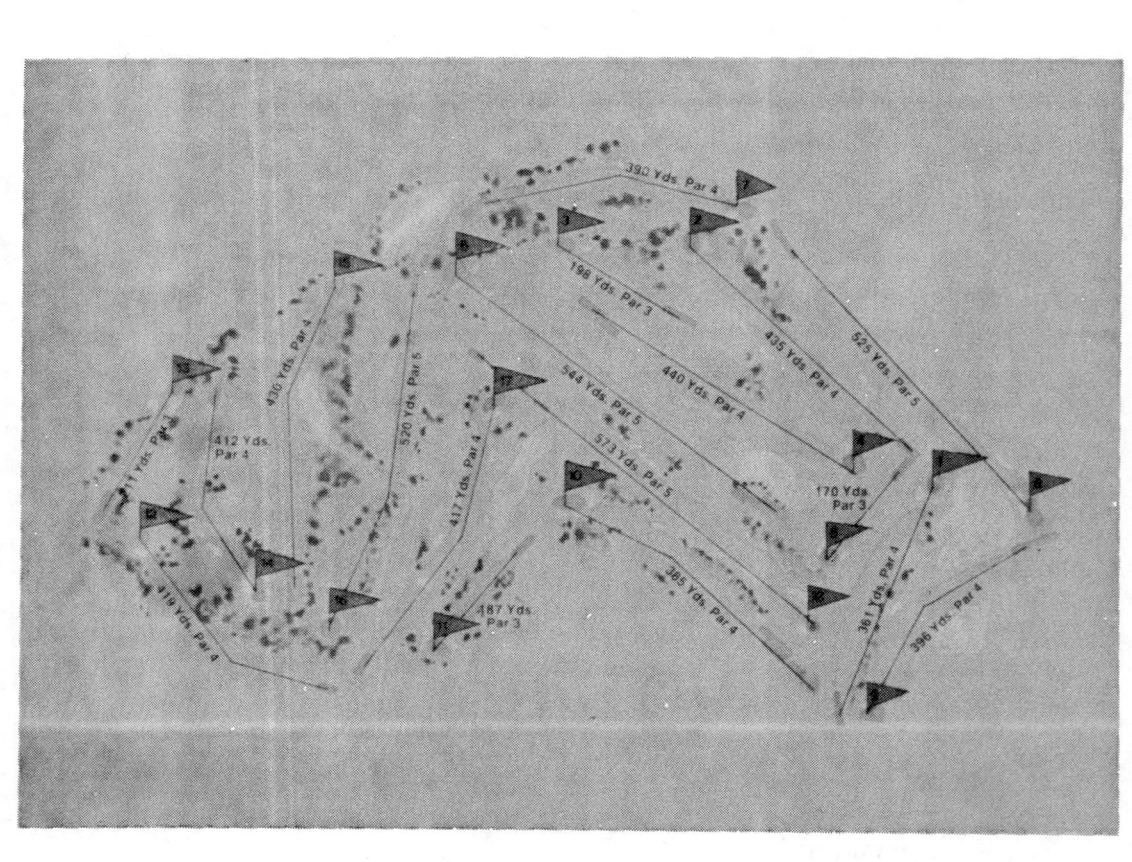

4

Site Analysis and Valuation

The site is land that has been improved for use as a golf course. In estimating its value the appraiser analyzes two distinct entities: the land and the improvements on the land. The land is valued first, and the value of the improvements is added to this estimate. Although they are joined physically, they are valued separately because the buildings and other improvements are a wasting asset. On a golf course the features that make it a golf course—for example, grading, landscaping, utilities, and irrigation system—are considered improvements along with the clubhouse and storage, maintenance, and other buildings.

HIGHEST AND BEST USE

The primary consideration in valuing golf course land is establishing highest and best use. An erroneous or unsupported selection of highest and best use, a common pitfall in appraising golf courses, is compounded in the calculations used to produce a final estimate of value. For example, in applying the market data approach, an incorrect premise could lead to erroneous selection of comparable sales which would lead to incorrect adjustment factors. In many appraisals the highest and best use of land is clearly the existing use. However, in the case of golf course properties, this may or may not be true. They are usually considered as special purpose properties; they are not so regularly sold or exchanged in the marketplace as most other properties; and zoning is usually as an exemption to a particular category since golf courses are often not in conformity with area use and density factors.

Golf courses are generally environmentally desirable, and this desirability causes a chain reaction in the community. The effect is seen in market activity of adjacent and proximate properties. Such land, which is in limited supply, may be in high demand, often for luxury residential use. Thus, a positive economic influence is created both in the community and on the golf course land itself.

Because of the continuing special market activity in and around golf courses and the activity's effect on valuation, the golf course appraiser should consider an analysis of the golf course land both on its existing use and on its reasonable, probable, and legal alternate highest and best use. Then the appraisal will be sufficiently convincing to enable a reader to determine that the highest and best use conclusion is proper and that the property was appraised in accordance with the purpose of the appraisal (usually market value).

The crucial thing to remember is that the golf course cannot be valued on the basis of one use for land and another for improvements. Unless the function of the appraisal is for determining an alternate use—for example, in a decision to use golf course land for residential sites—the highest and best use of the land is for a golf course as a going concern.

Even in the case of a golf course being appraised with the intention of changing its use to residential, the appraiser must conform to the theory of consistent use and remember that the improvements on the land might well dictate that the existing use will continue to be the highest and best use. Only when no value can be attributed to the improvements, or when they represent a negative value to the property, does an alternate use become the highest and best use.

The value of the land is estimated by comparing it to other open space land. The value of the improvements is then added to the land value estimate.

DATA REQUIREMENTS

As in all appraisals, an adequate land study for a golf course requires that pertinent types of data be assembled and considered. These include:

1. Title and record data
2. Taxes
3. Special assessments
4. Restrictions and easements
5. Legal description

Of particular importance in the analysis of the golf course site are:

1. Location
2. Accessibility
3. Zoning
4. Size and shape of site
5. Topography
6. Soil, drainage, and vegetation
7. Water and utilities

LOCATION

The weight of the location factor on the land value is often influenced by the type of golf course operation being appraised. A short course or daily-fee operation is best located where it is visible. It should be close to a population center with a few holes placed along a main thoroughfare for advertising purposes.

A private club need not be so obviously situated because visibility is not a consideration in its success. But it must be in a geographic area where there is a large enough population to support it through membership fees.

In resort areas the reciprocity between the golf course and surrounding land is especially noticeable. The golf course affects the value of surrounding land, which affects the value of the golf course. Often the resort is created by the golf courses. A good example is Pinehurst, North Carolina, which has 28 championship golf courses in a county with a population of about 42,000. Before the courses were built, raw land in the area sold for $200 to $300 per acre. Currently the value of large parcels of raw land contiguous to a golf course in the county ranges from $2,000 to $3,000 per acre. In addition, the presence of the golf courses has widened the types of adjacent and nearby land uses, which now include single family homes, condominiums, hotels, commercial use, and other recreational use.

A golf course that is near or part of a residential development can add perhaps $10,000 to the value of each unit abutting the course (see Figure

Figure 4.1. How a Golf Course Imparts Value to Surrounding Property

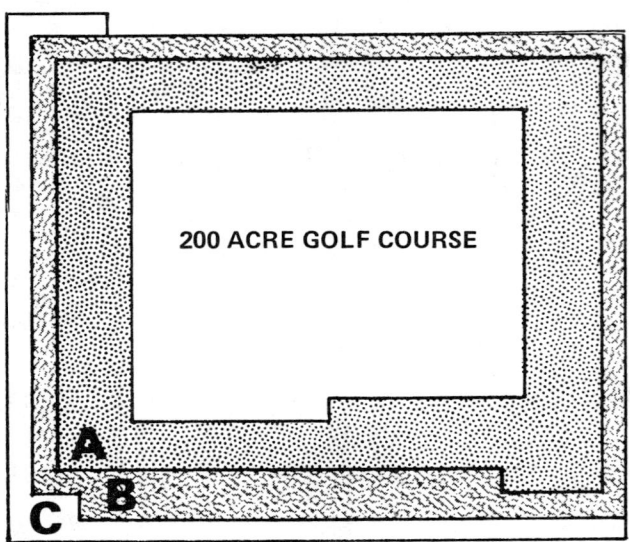

A. 200 one-acre lots worth $20,000 each
B. 100 one-acre lots worth $15,000 each
C. 50 one-acre lots worth $10,000 each

Reprinted with permission of the National Club Association from *Rising Property Taxes—Can Anything Be Done?*

4.1). Recognizing that this imparted value factor exists, the appraiser must be careful of how it is treated in the appraisal.

The following example shows how imparted value affects land near a golf course.[1] Assume an average residential neighborhood of 350 houses on one-acre lots. Included in the neighborhood is a 200-acre golf course. The 200 lots abutting the golf course are valued at $20,000 an acre. If the course did not exist, they would be worth only $10,000 an acre. Therefore, the value imparted to these lots by the course is $10,000 an acre. The 100 lots within a half-mile radius of the course are valued at $15,000 an acre; without the course, they would be only $10,000 an acre. The remaining 50 lots in the neighborhood receive no imparted value from the course and are valued at $10,000 an acre.

---

1. *Rising Property Taxes – Can Anything Be Done?* National Club Association Reference Series. (Washington, DC: National Club Association, 1976), p. 4-5.

The total value of residential property in the neighborhood is as follows:

200 lots at $20,000/acre	$4,000,000
100 lots at $15,000/acre	1,500,000
50 lots at $10,000/acre	500,000
Total value	$6,000,000

The average one-acre lot would be worth $17,142 ($6,000,000/350).

But if the golf course were replaced by residential development, there would be no imparted value to the 350 lots. Their total value would be as follows:

200 lots at $10,000/acre	$2,000,000
100 lots at $10,000/acre	1,000,000
50 lots at $10,000/acre	500,000
Total value	$3,500,000

The average one-acre lot would be worth $10,000 ($3,500,000/350).

Using a figure that includes the value imparted by the course to the surrounding land, the golf course's 200 acres would be worth $3,428,400 ($17,142 x 200). If the appraiser factored out the imparted value before making the required calculations, the course's land would then be worth $2,000,000 ($10,000 an acre). This represents a difference of $1,428,400.

ACCESSIBILITY

The quality of a golf course and its accessibility are inversely related—that is, accessibility has a higher effect on a low-quality course and a lower effect on a high-quality course. An avid golfer will search for a good course.

Accessibility is also more important to a daily-fee or municipal course than to a private club. A daily-fee course should be readily accessible, particularly if it is a small town course that is dependent on greens fees from transients to help meet maintenance costs.

Good transportation is necessary for club members. A golf club should be as near to town as the cost of land permits, and the main highway from town to club should be kept in good condition. An unpaved country lane that becomes impassable with every heavy rain is intolerable to members of a private club and could cause financial disaster to a daily-fee or municipal operation. In examining golf course income statements, the appraiser should be aware of accessibility as a factor in income. For example, a drop in receipts could have occurred during a period when the primary access road to the golf course was being repaved or was closed for some other reason.

Access for trucks and maintenance equipment must be provided both into the golf course and within its boundaries. Fertilizers and supplies must be trucked in, equipment must be serviced, and large mowing units and tractors must be driven from one hole to another. Bridges or roadways must be built to accommodate such heavy traffic. Often trees or other obstacles greatly restrict transportation between one portion of the course and another and create abnormal operational expense.

ZONING

The original three major zoning categories—residential, commercial, and industrial—are now being supplemented by many more sophisticated zones, such as overlay, historical, open space, and agricultural. Zoning for a golf course may be any of a number of uses, usually as an exemption to a particular category. Thus a course could be zoned as a residential exemption, commercial exemption, or industrial exemption. Golf courses have most often been zoned single family residential or, in the case of an outlying course, agricultural or recreational. Recently, however, they are increasingly zoned as open space land. This category includes undeveloped or semi-developed land parcels, which are usually more than five acres large. Land zoned as open space is limited to its existing use, which eliminates consideration of the golf course site for a more productive alternate use.

The possibility of a zoning change to permit an alternative use is a consideration in the site analysis. Economic demand for a higher use could be an issue that would influence a decision for such a change; or contrarily, there may be social pressure to preserve the land as open space.

The zoning category and permitted accessory uses under that category are stated in the appraisal report. Also specified are building and site restrictions: maximums allowed for building height and building coverage and minimums for lot size, lot width, front yard, side yards, and rear yard. The appraiser specifies that the property conforms to zoning ordinances and indicates any variances.

SIZE AND SHAPE OF SITE

The National Golf Foundation specifies minimum sizes for 9- and 18-hole golf courses: 50 acres for a 9-hole course and 110 acres for an 18-hole course. Safety of golfers playing parallel holes prescribes larger minimum areas: 80 acres for a 9-hole course and 160 acres for an 18-hole course. Groups of large trees or woodlands can help to segregate fairways, reducing needed acreage to a certain extent. Proximity of residential units should also be considered in land requirement analysis.

Less land is required if the terrain is flat; on heavily rolling land up to 15% more acreage may be required. There must be sufficient north-south yardage to eliminate holes facing the sun. Championship 7,000-yard play can seldom be accommodated on fewer than 140 acres. Merion, Pennsylvania, has the only famous championship course in the country with fewer than 200 acres; most championship courses are built on 200 to more than 300 acres. (See Chapter 1 for the acreage requirements for the various configurations for play.)

The ideal shape for a golf course site is rectangular. A course that is part of a residential development could be developed most effectively on a block rather than strung out through a subdivision where roads would take up an inordinate proportion of the designated land. A "strung-out" design, however, would provide many additional lots abutting the fairways.

The design of the course again comes into focus in regard to size and shape of the site. Less land is required for a well-designed course; maintenance crews can work more efficiently; and distances do not seem so great to golfers. An irregularly shaped site can be suitable for use as a golf course and can be developed into an interesting layout by a creative golf course architect.

TOPOGRAPHY

Gently rolling terrain is perfect for a golf course. It should not be so hilly or rugged that players would tire easily or be forced to use golf carts, that it would be unsafe for golf cart travel, that many blind shots would be required, or that cost of construction and maintenance would be unreasonable. Natural golf features—creek valleys, woodlands, ravines, ponds—are an asset to a site, but they are not a necessity since they can be added. Flat land can be bulldozed to build up knolls; and although rivers, creeks, and ponds can serve as a natural water supply, water can be piped in. Trees on the site add to the aesthetics of the golf course.

SOIL, DRAINAGE, AND VEGETATION

The composition, depth, and condition of the soil on the site are of primary importance because the turf raised on fairways and greens is the ultimate requirement for a good golf course. The ideal soil for greens is six-inch deep sandy loam, which should be in top condition. If the soil's natural plant food is depleted, large amounts of fertilization will be needed for proper cultivation of turf.

The soil can be analyzed inexpensively by state agricultural departments or county agricultural agents. State agricultural experiment stations and county agents can also provide information on proper turf development and proper grass seeding, growing, and maintenance.

Some technical deficiencies on golf courses are caused by seedbed problems. Using existing native soil that is improper for turf cultivation is initially inexpensive but becomes quite costly. Poor soil structure, inadequate drainage, and heavy and concentrated traffic cause compaction, a problem that can originate unnoticed and become progressively severe. Unless maintenance actions are taken, compaction will eventually destroy the turf.

Drainage must be adequate to prevent standing water, which often necessitates the installation of tiles. A high, dry site is sometimes preferable to swampy, low land because of the added construction costs for earthmoving and drainage.

Selection of the correct species or varieties of grass seed or stolons for the particular soil and climate is extremely important. Hybrid Bermudagrasses, which are planted from stolons, or scattered vegetative pieces of grass are used on golf courses in warm to tropical climates. Seeded varieties are generally used in cool season areas or transition zones. Penncross or Emerald Creeping Bentgrass would be used on greens. Various mixtures of the improved Kentucky bluegrasses, turf-type perennial ryegrasses, and/or fescues would be used on tees, fairways, and roughs. Certified seed is used to ensure quality and purity.

Planting trees or retention of existing trees when site clearing occurs is very important. Strategically placed trees, properly planted, can add considerably to the value of a golf course. They define fairways, serve as hazards, offer shade, and increase the beauty of a course. Trees in the wrong place can interfere with play, cause excessive shading which is detrimental to turf growth, compete with turf for soil nutrients, or create undue maintenance problems. Improper selection of varieties can cause undesirable litter or root problems, and poor spacing and positioning of trees can cause both maintenance and playing problems.

The National Association of Arborists offers a tree valuation schedule. The correct tree in the correct location on a particular hole can add greatly to the value of that hole. Rare or imported trees add more value than native species, and mature trees are usually more valuable than young ones. When used correctly, however, a mix of both is an asset to a golf course.

WATER AND UTILITIES

Water, sewers, and electricity are necessities on a golf course. The source of water must be close to the golf course and pure enough to drink and irrigate the turf. Ponds and lakes can be utilized aesthetically, strategically, and for water retention for maintenance. According to the National Golf Foundation, the amount of water needed during the playing season may be projected on the basis of 1 inch per week on fairways and about 1½ to 2 inches per week on greens. The quality of the water must also be checked. Problems with the turf as well as the irrigation system can be caused by water that is high in acid or sulfur content.

Electric power will be needed for irrigation, the clubhouse, and to charge electric golf carts. Cost includes running lines from the source of commerical power and the cost per kilowatt-hour for use. Natural gas, gasoline, and diesel fuel are also used, both to power pumps and generate electricity.

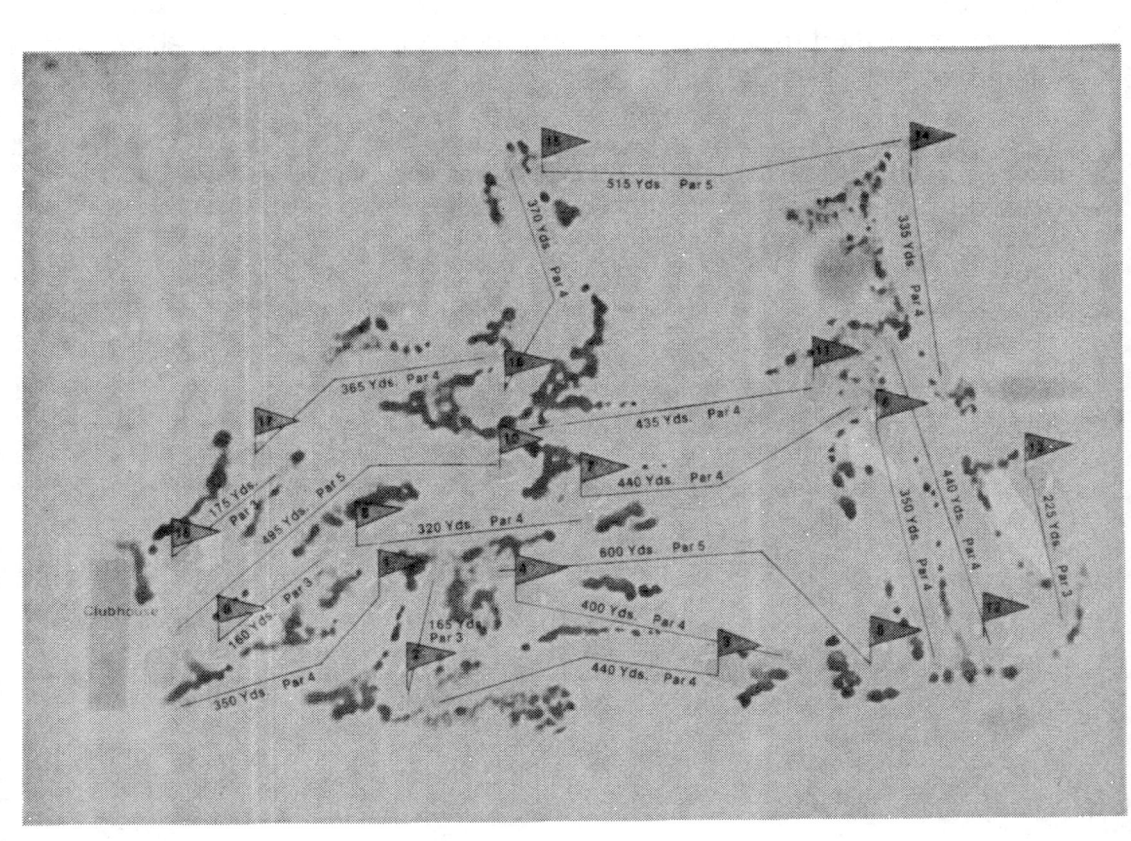

5
Golf Course Improvements

Each golf course is unique. Because golfers are competing with themselves against the course, its distinctive characteristics entice the golfer to challenge it. But the very singularity of a golf course makes the appraiser's job difficult. There are so many variables that even "ball park" cost figures are impossible to state, and only general parameters can be given to help the appraiser. High, low, and median development costs derived from a study of 20 golf facilities opened during 1977 appear on the following page (Table 5.1). These figures, however, cannot be construed as "average" and applied to a golf course being appraised. Ultimately each course must be personally inspected; its playability must be judged; and the contribution to value of each element must be considered.

The playability of a golf course is greatly dependent on overall design. The "model" course has a good proportion of the three types of holes: penal, strategic, and heroic. *Penal* holes are those in which sand traps guard the greens in bottleneck, or island, fashion and force the golfer to shoot accurately or play short. Penal design is usually found on one or two short holes on an 18-hole course. *Strategic* holes, about half the holes on modern golf courses, have fewer traps, but they are well-placed. The golfer can hit at full power but must place the shots. *Heroic* holes are a combination of penal and strategic design. Hazards are placed diagonally, and the golfer shoots accordingly. About 30 to 50% of holes are heroic.

Table 5.1. Golf Facility Development Costs, 1977*

	High	Low	Median
Golf course development costs			
Basic golf course construction (clearing, grading, construction of tees, greens, and traps, seeding, etc.)	$1,500,000	$150,000	$ 410,287
Irrigation system	300,000	88,243	160,000
Pump house	35,000	2,000	13,555
Cart paths, shelters, bridges, etc	100,000	10,000	40,000
Service road	14,800	1,000	5,000
Maintenance equipment	120,000	62,141	84,710
Maintenance building	119,767	12,500	42,500
Pre-opening maintenance	130,000	20,000	45,000
Total	$2,319,567	$345,884	$ 801,052
Clubhouse and golf cart costs			
Clubhouse construction	$ 789,276	$ 50,000	$ 240,000
Clubhouse equipment and furnishings	177,084	2,000	60,000
Entrance road and parking	80,000	3,000	38,900
Golf carts (median of 39 carts)	90,000	28,000	54,000
Golf cart storage shelter	90,000	6,000	50,000
Total	$1,226,360	$ 89,000	$ 442,900
Total facility development costs	$3,545,927	$434,884	$1,243,952

* Costs do not include land acquisition costs or architect's fees.

Source: "Golf Market Report" (North Palm Beach, FL: National Golf Foundation), August 1978.

Design standards include number of par 3, par 4, and par 5 holes; length of holes; and placement of holes.

With a par of 35, 36, or 37, the recommended distribution of holes for each nine is two par 3s, two par 5s, and five par 4s. Par 6 holes are to be avoided. A suggested order is 4-5-4-3-4-5-4-3-4. The order is repeated on the second nine of an 18-hole course.

The United States Golf Association has established the following par-to-yardage relationships.

	Men	Women
Par 3	Under 250 yards	Under 210 yards
Par 4	251-470 yards	211-400 yards
Par 5	Over 471 yards	401-575 yards

Yardage listed on scorecards is not always accurate (particularly on par 5 holes and to a lesser degree on par 4s and par 3s), so the careful appraiser measures a few representative holes. If there is a discrepancy between stated and actual yardage, all holes must be checked.

Well-planned placement of holes enhances play. The first and tenth holes should be easy par 4 holes from 380 to 400 yards long. Two par 3 holes per nine are preferably the fourth and eighth holes. East-to-west holes are to be avoided, and a southwest direction is particularly bad. The walk from the green of one hole to the tee of the next should be less than 75 yards, and the preferred distance is 20 to 30 yards. The first and tenth tees and the sixth, ninth, and eighteenth greens are best located near the clubhouse to provide the greatest convenience for golfers. A practice tee, fairway, and green near the clubhouse is now an expected addition.

For valuation, golf course improvements are treated in two categories: improvements to the land and buildings. Land improvements include:

Tees
Greens
Fairways
Roughs
Hazards
Watering systems

Golf cart paths and bridges
Practice facilities
Parking lots

Buildings include:

Clubhouse
Maintenance building
Storage buildings
Miscellaneous structures

LAND IMPROVEMENTS

In determining the cost of land improvements, the appraiser must be cognizant of the wide range that exists. A well-known architect who designs elaborate golf courses might say that the cost to build 18 holes is from $900,000 to $1,500,000 ($50,000 to about $83,500 per hole). Yet some daily fee operators are currently building 18 holes for from $215,000 to $270,000 ($12,000 to $15,000 per hole), and some architects are building for around $15,000 per hole. The costs to build shown in the following sections are *ranges* and are shown to give the appraiser an idea of relative values only. In areas where union labor is required, materials must be trucked, or other conditions exist to affect costs, the figures could vary considerably.

Tees

The golfer starts each hole at the tee, generally pushing a wooden or plastic tee, from which the ball is hit, into the ground.

Tee areas should be well defined, flat on top, well covered with closely mowed turf, and based on a good soil that will take a tee easily and resist compaction. New courses are using a modified greens soil mix to a depth of 6 to 14 inches. Openings through trees abutting the tee should be wide enough to allow air movement and sunshine for a healthy turf. For drainage, tees should be sloped 1% in any direction but always away from the bench or cart path area. They should be gently sloped on the sides to allow for maintenance with power equipment. Often the most abused part of the golf course, tees should be maintained with the same care given to greens, and growth for recovery should be continuously encouraged. Tees, like greens, should be irrigated.

Ideally, at least two separate tee areas are provided for each hole. They should be large enough to enable the superintendent to switch the tee markers around to distribute wear and preserve the turf. Adequate size is also essential to accommodate the anticipated traffic. A rule of thumb is to provide a minimum of 100 square feet of tee surface for each 1,000 rounds of play. Many golf course architects indicate that minimum size of a tee should be 5,000 square feet.

Common deficiencies observed on tees are:

- Area is too small.
- Surface is uneven or poorly sloped.
- Sides are so steep that hand maintenance is required.
- Soil is too heavy, making compaction a major problem.
- Heavy vegetation and trees provide too much shade and restrict air movement.
- Poor access for golfers creates adverse traffic patterns and paths or worn turf.
- Location of tees is hazardous, and golfers risk being hit by an errant golf shot.
- Poor drainage impedes play and causes compaction.

A tee that is merely a closely mowed area at one end of a fairway would cost little or nothing. An elevated tee, with proper soil mixture and subsurface drainage tile that is properly designed and constructed, would cost about 25¢ to $1 a square foot for new construction. Cost for building a new tee on an existing course would be around $1 a square foot.[1]

Greens

A green is an irregularly shaped area of as nearly perfect turf as possible where the golfer finishes the hole and putts the ball into the cup. The green should be elevated for visibility, sloping toward the approach area so that the location of sand traps and other hazards is evident to the golfer trying to place the ball on the green. The slope should also provide for drainage in at least two directions. A contoured surface creates interest and helps the golfer to predict the ball's path. The contours should allow 70% of the putting

---

1. These amounts will vary according to locality, soil conditions, terrain, type of facility, and other factors.

surface for cup or pin (flag) placement positions to vary the difficulty and distribute wear. Each pin placement location, in the center of a circle with a three-foot radius, should be relatively level so the cup will not be in the side of a small hill.

Proper size of greens depends on anticipated traffic and difficulty of the individual hole. An exceptionally large green on a short hole could be undesirable. Greens should be large enough to provide a good target and small enough to discourage too-long "monster shots." Sizes range from 3,000 to 10,000 square feet, with average size being 5,000 to 6,000 square feet.

The composition of the soil must be such that it drains well and is not subject to compaction. Construction of greens varies from a flat mowed area on a farm course to a raised mound of native soil to an architecturally designed U.S.G.A. green. Three types of greens construction are shown in Figure 5.1. The first type, partial modification of soil, has a layer of coarse sand over subsoil (see Figure 5.1a). The top layer is sandy loam soil 12 inches deep. Drainage is through the subsoil. Such a green can be built at a cost of about $1 a square foot.

A U.S.G.A. green has a 12-inch soil mix (about 85% sand and 15% peat), over a two-inch layer of coarse sand, over a four-inch layer of gravel, over subsoil graded 1% toward four-inch tiles at ten-foot intervals (see Figure 5.1b). The soil layer accepts water until it almost puddles. When the weight of the water breaks the surface tension, there is a sudden flush that pulls the water through the coarse sand and gravel into the tile, which carries it away. The cost of an architecturally designed and properly installed U.S.G.A. green is approximately $20,000.

An appraiser who is told that greens were constructed according to U S.G.A. specifications should question whether composition samples were sent to the U.S.G.A. for analysis. The U.S.G.A. greens section method is not a "do-it-yourself" project. The particle sizes in each layer must be exactly correct to produce the desired drainage effect.

Designed and patented by Bill Daniels of Purdue University, the Purr-Wick green (see Figure 5.1c) is built in terraces, with a four-inch lip on each terrace and a drain tile through each. At the end of each terrace is a riser that regulates the height of the water and therefore the moisture content of the soil mix. The soil mix is basically the same as that on a U.S.G.A. green. The advantage of this scientifically designed soil system is that a good superintendent can force grass with roots at a rate of three to four inches a week. Starting with bare soil, a green can be covered with healthy turf with 12-inch-deep roots within about three weeks. The cost of a Purr-Wick green is around $20,000, about the same as a U.S.G.A. green.

Figure 5.1. Greens Construction—Cross Sections

a. Partial Modification of Soil

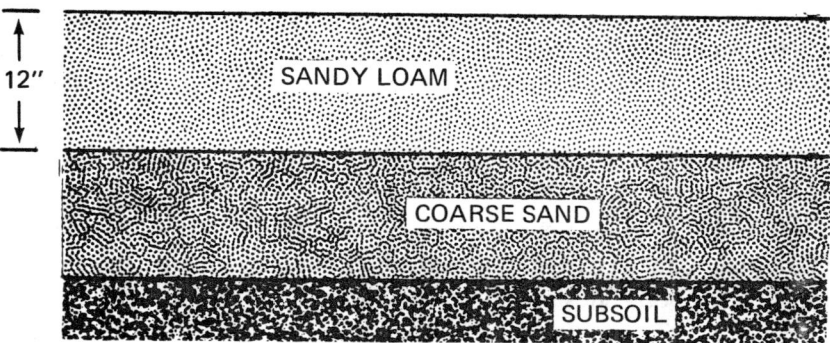

b. U.S.G.A. Greens Section Method

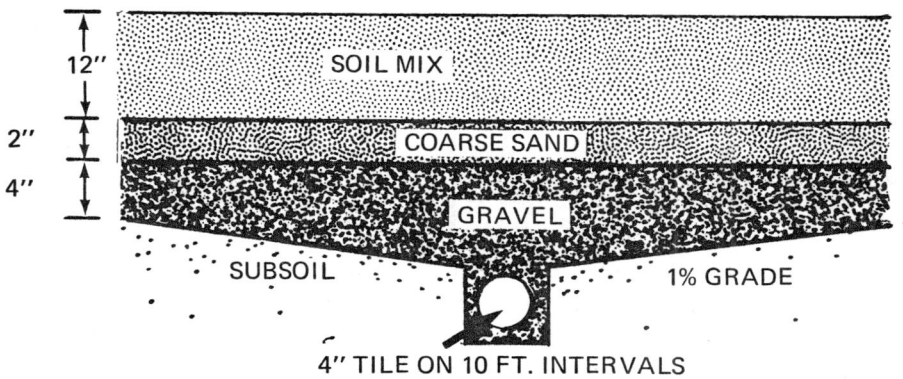

c. Purr-Wick

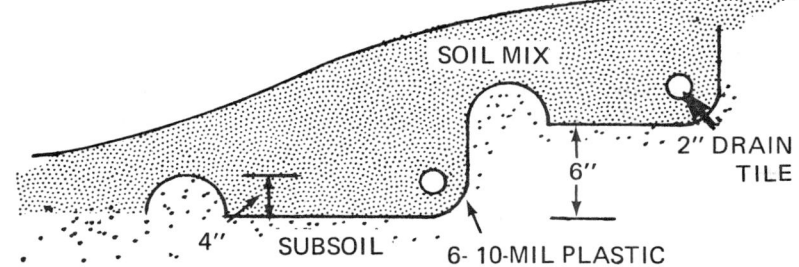

Common problems that adversely affect the value of a green are:
- Green is not elevated for visibility, but is merely a closely mowed area.
- Slope is improper, either too steep or away from pockets that trap water.
- Soil structure is incorrect. Too much clay causes compaction problems; too much sand causes leaching problems; and rocks in the subsoil interfere with cup placements. Improper soil mix depth causes localized dry spots.
- Landscaping or trees near the green block sunlight or hinder air movement.
- Steep side banks cause maintenance problems.
- Poor approaches create traffic wear.
- Putting area is too large or too small.

Cost of greens can vary from about 50¢ to about $2 a square foot. A flat green on native soil would be at the low end of the range; and an elevated, properly designed, constructed, and drained green of scientifically designed soil mixture, built to U.S.G.A. or Purr-Wick specifications, would be closer to $2 a square foot.[2]

The quality of greens construction can indicate the quality of an entire course since there is usually a similar level of quality throughout. If the greens are poorly constructed, no doubt the tees and fairways are also poorly constructed. Looking at a typical hole on a golf course and learning if the greens cost was $2,000, say, or $75,000 can help to establish a range of value for the entire course.

Fairways

The fairway is the area between the tee and green where a golfer hopes the ball will travel. From tee to green is not, however, necessarily a straight line. A fairway, which must be wide enough to be fair and narrow enough to provide a challenge, is shaped somewhat like a trapezoid.

The path along the fairway from tee to green must be visible, and the turf must be able to hold the ball up properly and be soft enough so a golf club can take a divot[3] if required. Drainage must be adequate to prevent wet spots; and contouring must be smooth enough to accommodate mowing and have enough access for large gang mowers. A well-designed fairway has definite boundaries, is not too hilly, and is rock-free.

The most common problems seen on fairways are:

---

2. These amounts will vary according to locality, soil conditions, terrain, type of facility, and other factors.
3. A piece of turf dug from the fairway in making a shot.

- Improper drainage hinders playability.
- Lack of width makes play overly difficult.
- Excessive roughness causes difficult lies, bumps, or unpredictable bounces of the golf ball.
- Soil is too hard, so a divot cannot be taken.
- Boundaries are poorly defined, confusing the golfer about direction of play.
- Poor bridges or steep hills make travel difficult or hazardous.
- Outcroppings of rocks damage clubs and mowing equipment.
- Poor turf increases maintenance requirements and impedes play.

A fairway may be extremely simple—a mowed area of former pastureland. Or it may be very elaborate—an area carved through woods and swamps requiring considerable earth moving and tree removal with tiles for drainage and bridges for travel. Or, typically, a fairway is something between the two extremes. Cost varies from $75 to $2,000 an acre. A good-sized regulation golf course contains from 40 to 90 acres of maintained fairways.[4]

Roughs

The 10- to 40-foot wide areas on each side of a fairway, which are intended to guide a golfer and set the direction for play, are the roughs. The character of a rough is similar to the fairway, but with slightly longer grass. If the grass is too long, golf balls are hard to find and shots out of them are extremely difficult.

Maintenance of roughs should be easy. Small areas around trees should be treated with chemicals to eliminate grass and thus hand trimming, and trees should be spaced so that larger mowing equipment can be used.

Most courses use a lower-quality turf in the rough areas. However, some large clubs may irrigate, fertilize, and provide a high degree maintenance for the roughs.

Common problems are:

- Roughs that are merely native pastureland may be bumpy and full of holes and weeds.
- An abundance of trees, brush, or rocks complicates maintenance.

---

4. These amounts will vary according to locality, soil conditions, terrain, type of facility, and other factors.

- Wet areas that have never been drained cause play and maintenance problems.
- Clumpy and thin turf results from an unsuitable seed mix.

A rough that is an unimproved part of what was originally pastureland would have no significant value, but one that is built, irrigated, and maintained like a fairway would have value that is comparable to a fairway. Most roughs would be valued at around $100 an acre.[5]

Hazards

Sand bunkers (traps), ponds, and other obstacles to play are classified as hazards. They should not be too tough or make a hole too tricky, but they should present a challenge to players of all levels of ability. As for all elements on a golf course, design, location, and construction of hazards should be planned with consideration toward maintenance.

Sand bunkers are usually used to outline greens, direct play, hold errant shots, or increase the strategic value of holes. Properly placed where they will penalize a poor shot but not interfere with a good one, good-quality bunkers are irregularly shaped with capes of turf extending into them to allow easy ingress and egress. The best sand traps are usually cut into the face of the mound rather than being merely a depression in the ground. They contain a six-inch layer of loose sand that will neither readily pack nor blow away. The sides are sloped for easy maintenance, and they are kept free of weeds and standing water. Although too many sand bunkers on a golf course slow play and increase maintenance costs, 36 to 54 bunkers on a public course add interest and increase play.

Value-decreasing defects are:

- Water hazards are positioned so that they require a long "carry" over the water or short lay-up shots.
- Weeds and algae are allowed to grow in water hazards, making them eyesores.
- Bunkers are too tall, too steep, and weed infested, which makes them hard to maintain.
- Traps are too flat and are not visible.
- Poor drainage causes traps to hold water.

---

5. This amount will vary according to locality, soil conditions, terrain, type of facility, and other factors.

- Difficult shape impedes maintenance.
- Location handicaps average golfer.
- Sand is hard packed or contains stones.

Water hazards are a tremendously variable item. Recent estimates of the cost of ponds are around $2,000 each, but their cost is affected by difficulty of excavation; lining, which may be plastic, cement, or asphalt; and unique design characteristics.

A sand trap that is well constructed and properly drained, with a built-up bunker behind it, may cost $500 to $1,000 near a green. A fairway trap with proper buildup and drainage could cost $5,000.[6] Some experts suggest that a misplaced, poorly drained sand trap with the wrong kind of sand has a negative value because it is worse than none at all; others argue that any existing trap is a distinctive feature of a golf hole and should not be considered to have negative value.

Watering Systems

The variables to be considered in determining the watering requirements on a golf course include climate, topography, soil texture, wind and temperature conditions, vegetation, solar intensity, water source and its cost, turfgrass varieties, cost of electricity, and area labor costs. Agronomists recommend that for proper turf growth the top four inches of soil be kept moist. Because only a few areas of the country have adequate year-round rainfall to maintain continuous recommended moisture, watering systems are required on most golf courses, at least for tees and greens and usually for fairways as well.

In the past a common method of watering was to attach a hose and portable sprinkler to an outlet at each green. Now manual, semi-automatic, or fully automatic systems, utilizing quick-couple sprinklers, pop-ups, or a combination of the two, are used for irrigation. In-place pipelines with outlets in fairways or around greens and tees are utilized for a quick-couple system. Rotating sprinkler heads can be manually inserted for watering. Pop-ups are sprinkler heads recessed in the ground, which can be raised by electrical or hydraulic pressure for watering. Control of pop-ups can range from manual to highly complex computer control.

---

6. These amounts will vary according to locality, soil conditions, terrain, type of facility, and other factors.

The amount of water needed will dictate the best system for the individual course. Some general facts can help in the choice of a system that is neither superadequate nor inadequate. Average soil absorbs one-quarter inch of water per hour. However, sprinkler heads for turf irrigation apply water at a much higher rate, and precipitation rate in inches per hour is usually figured by the following formulas.[7]

For triangular spacing: $\dfrac{\text{GPM} \times 96.3}{\text{Spacing}^2 \times .866}$

For square spacing: $\dfrac{\text{GPM} \times 96.3}{\text{Spacing}^2}$

For single-row spacing: $\dfrac{\text{GPM} \times 96.3}{\text{distance between scallops} \times \text{spacing}}$

The water supply can be either ponds and retention basins or wells. If the surface water is fed by a stream or river, water rights may be required. Before well water can be used, its mineral and chemical content must be checked.

Either centrifugal or turbine pumps are used for an irrigation system. The type and size is determined by the water source and watering requirements.

Cost of an irrigation system has been estimated at one-third or more of the costs of construction for the entire course. A range of $50,000 to $300,000, depending on degree of automation of the systems and what parts of the course are to be irrigated, is not uncommon.[8] Table 5.2 shows the range of costs for an irrigation system for 18 holes with a pumping plant from surface water supply and 180-ft.-diameter fairway sprinklers. The costs shown would be reasonable for the Midwest and most of the country. Table 5.3 shows multiplication factors for specific features of the system shown in Table 5.2.

---

7. *Planning and Building the Golf Course* (North Palm Beach, FL: National Golf Foundation, n.d.), p. 25.
8. These amounts will vary according to locality, soil conditions, terrain, type of facility, and other factors.

Table 5.2. Range of Costs for Irrigation System for 18 Holes

Quick-coupling valve system	$100,000 — $120,000
Quick-coupling fairway with automatic tee and green system	$115,000 — $130,000
Single-row automatic fairway (valve-in-head), tee, and green system	$140,000 — $170,000
Dual-row automatic fairway, tee, and green system	$160,000 — $250,000

Source: Douglas A. Bruce, PE, Johns-Manville Sales Corporation, Fresno, CA.

Table 5.3. Multiplication Factors for Specific Features

9-hole vs. 18-hole	− 40%
600-800 vs. 1,000-1,200 GPM pumping plant	− 20%
Central control of the automatic controllers	+ $5,000 to $10,000
Hydraulic valve-in-head vs. electric valve-in-head control	− 20%
Class-200 PVC pipe vs. class-160 PVC	+ 3%
Transite pipe vs. class-160 PVC (3″ or 4″ and larger)	+ 5%
Valve under head vs. valve in head	+ 5%
Tees longer than 120′ (men's) or 60′ (women's)	$250 each tee
Tees in excess of 1 men's and 1 women's per hole	$500 each tee
C.I. or brass vs. plastic sprinklers (includes valve under head)	+ 10%
150′- to 160′-diameter fairway sprinklers vs. 180′ (single row)	− 10%
Battery system for fairways vs. valve in head	no factor
90′-fairway sprinkler spacing vs. 80′	− 15%

Source: Douglas A. Bruce, PE, Johns-Manville Sales Corporation, Fresno, CA.

In the arid parts of the country, such as Arizona and California, three-row and fence-to-fence coverage systems are common. The 18-hole installations cost around $400,000, but prices fluctuate 20% depending on area of coverage and specific features of the systems.

Golf Cart Paths and Bridges

Golf cart paths are a virtual necessity on golf courses that are heavily played. They may be designated grass paths or narrow roadways constructed of materials ranging from dirt to concrete. The paths may be constructed only in high-traffic areas or may be continuous throughout the course. The decision to build partial or continuous paths depends on climate, terrain, and the type of soil that predominates on the course. Continuous paths are most common in areas that have a hilly terrain or heavy soil that is subject to compaction and where wet climatic conditions prevail. Partial paths may be sufficient if the soil is resistant to compaction, wet weather is less frequent, and terrain is relatively flat.

Bridges may be simple culverts or aesthetically pleasing, covered structures. Attractive bridges are an asset, but function is most important. Some must be sturdy enough to accommodate heavy maintenance equipment as well as foot and golf cart traffic. They must be designed and maintained for safety.

Practice Facilities

A practice area—a tee, green, and fairway—has become an expected part of a good golf course. Design, construction, and turf should be commensurate with the design, construction, and turf of the regular holes on the course. The total area should be from 250 to 300 yards long, with the tee area large enough to move the tee markers frequently to avoid severe maintenance problems.

Practice facilities are often used during twilight and early evening hours, so they require a lighting system. General-purpose, weatherproof, enclosed floodlights are recommended. They should be placed on 25- to 30-foot high poles for greatest efficiency. Tables 5.4 and 5.5 show capacities and other elements related to lighting.

BUILDINGS

Among the buildings on a golf course, the clubhouse and maintenance building are the two that have characteristics unique to this type of property.

Clubhouses

An adequate clubhouse is comprised of a medium-sized pro shop, snack bar, banquet rooms, and men's and women's locker rooms. The range from ade-

Table 5.4. Golf Course Lights

Poles Req.	Height	Type	Fixtures Required	Watts KVA	Type	Footcandle Level
5	20"	Quartz	20	30	1500 W. Quartz	8 Footcandles on tee
5	30"	Mercury vapor	15	16.2	1000 W. Mercury vapor	4 Vertical footcandles at 600 ft. 2 Vertical footcandles at 900 ft.
5	30"	Metalic vapor	15	16.2	1000 W. Metalic vapor	15 Footcandles on tee 7 Vertical footcandles at 600 ft. 3 Vertical footcandles at 900 ft.

Source: *Golf Driving Range Manual* (North Palm Beach, FL. National Golf Foundation 1978).

Table 5.5. How To Select the Fixture

Type	Output	Life	Cost	Color
Quartz	Medium	2,000 hrs.	Low	Excellent
Mercury	High	24,000 hrs.	High	Fair to good
Metal	Highest	7,500 hrs.	Highest	Good

Source: *Golf Driving Range Manual* (North Palm Beach, FL: National Golf Foundation, 1978).

quate to luxurious is enormous. An exclusive country club that provides space for social functions and other recreational activities may include in the main clubhouse locker and shower facilities, massage rooms, saunas and steam rooms, restaurants, cocktail lounges, indoor swimming pool, beauty parlor, barber shop, bowling alleys, and activity rooms. In addition, their facilities may include residences for pros and managers, putting greens, driving ranges, tennis courts, hotel rooms, riding paths, or a boat marina.

Cost of a clubhouse varies, of course, according to type of facility and materials used in construction. Reproduction cost, combined with an estimate of accrued depreciation, is used to value improvements by the cost approach. Average cost data tables are available through various construction cost services. If such tables are used, the appraiser will have to adjust for specific structural variations between the service's base structure and the clubhouse being appraised as well as for the market area and time.

The floor plans of the two-story clubhouse at Arlington Lakes Golf Club, Arlington Heights, Illinois, appear on the following pages.[9]

Maintenance Buildings

For maximum efficiency, the National Golf Foundation recommends that a modern maintenance complex should be designed to include:

1. Storage for machinery and supplies
2. Facilities for construction, painting, and repairs
3. Administrative office for the superintendent

The complex should be located on flat ground for ease in maneuvering machines and mixing and storing topdressing. The area should be well drained, be accessible to large trucks and for utility hookups, and be out of range of errant golf balls.

The building should be large enough to store all machinery and materials and accommodate a repair shop and personnel area. A center aisle and large doors at each end are preferable, but if the building is not wide enough

---

9. This golf course, designed by the David Gill Corporation, St. Charles, IL, opened for play June 1, 1979. The clubhouse as well as the maintenance and storage building were designed by Wendt, Cedarholm & Tippens, Architects, Northbrook, IL.

Table 5.6 Square Footage for Specific Areas

Equipment and fertilizer storage area	6,000 sq. ft.
Mechanical repair shop	1,300 sq. ft.
Employee locker room	300 sq. ft.
Restroom (optional shower)	100 sq. ft.
Superintendent's office	300 sq. ft.
Steam cleaning and paint room	300 sq. ft.
Fireproof oil and grease storage room	100 sq. ft.
Total floor space	8,400 sq. ft.

Source: "Planning the Golf Course Maintenance Building," Information Sheet GC-27 (North Palm Beach, FL: National Golf Foundation, n.d.).

for this plan, it should have several doors opening from the side. A minimum width of 12 to 14 feet is recommended for overhead doors, and a height of 10 to 12 feet is best for semi-trailer entrances. Doors should not be on the north or windy side of the building.

Lighting in all work areas must be good, and at least the workshop and office areas should be heated and insulated. A floor drain for the washing-cleaning area is recommended, and the arc welding and spraying area should be separated from the other areas. Gas pumps should be located where they do not block normal traffic flow, but they must be accessible for large machines. An overhead rail that will hold a half-ton hoist should be provided for handling vehicle engines and large mowers.

The maximum square footage as recommended by the National Golf Foundation for specific areas in the maintenance building is shown in Table 5.6. For more than 18 holes, the recommended floor space requirements should be increased by 50% for each room (except for the golf course superintendent's office, for which 300 sq. ft. is adequate).

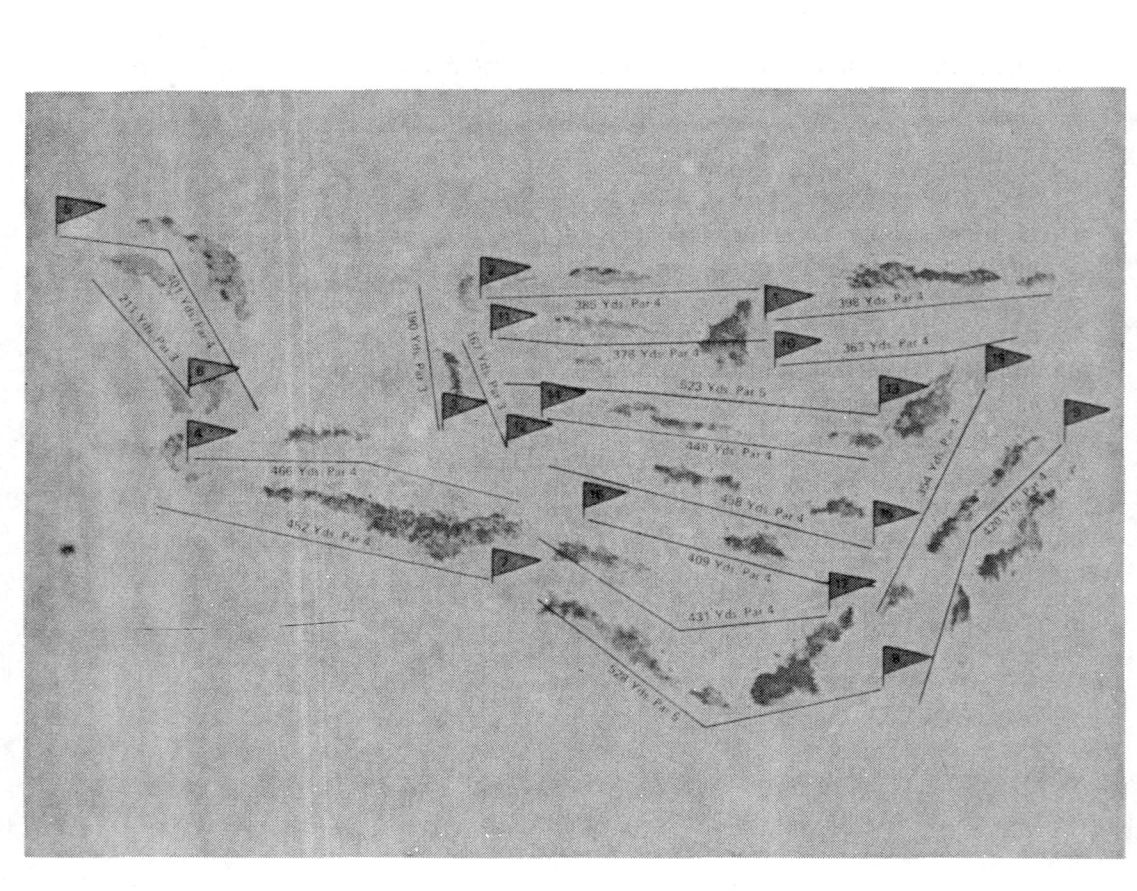

6

Golf Course Operations

Analysis of the operations of nonprofit private golf clubs owned and operated solely to benefit members differs from analysis of profit-making private, semiprivate, or public courses owned by individual investors, hotels, or motels.

Many nonprofit private clubs show a deficit after paying all operating and fixed expenses and providing for replacement reserves and/or rehabilitation. Payroll costs often increase without an offsetting increase in dues, sales, or other income. Clubs have not been able to solve financial problems by raising or lowering restaurant and bar prices. Some have tried buffet service in the dining room to cut expenses; others have hired professional managers for more economic operation and have added other facilities, such as bowling alleys and swimming pools, to attract more member use. Many clubs remain solvent only by periodic pro rata assessment of members.

With public courses, the municipality usually attempts to recover operating costs, but income is seldom sufficient for economic return on the investment or to compensate for lost real estate tax revenue. Operating budgets for municipal courses may not be available because they are often part of a city or county's overall park and recreation budget.

However, the golf course industry is changing rapidly. Not too long ago almost all golf courses, like country clubs and municipal courses, were nonprofit ventures, with insufficient income for return on investment. Today, however, more than half of all new golf courses are daily-fee businesses, many private clubs are sold to investors, and even some municipal courses are leased to profit-oriented operators. In the past, because of the nonprofit nature of the industry, appraisers gave little weight to the income approach in the valuation of golf courses. In view of the current trend toward operating a golf course for profit, a close analysis of income and expenses is now an important aspect of the valuation process of this kind of property.

INCOME

The amount of golf course income is highly variable according to the type of facility, location, season, and clientele. Some clubs are able to run a successful food and bar business, but most are not. In some areas of the country, clubs have an extremely high golf cart revenue, but in others they have almost none. Driving ranges vary from a non-revenue-producing practice area to an elaborate heated and covered area producing $100,000 or more per year in revenue.

Sources of income are determined by the type of course. For private clubs the main sources are membership dues, house charges, assessments, initiation fees, and greens fees. Municipal and public daily-fee courses have greens fees, and semiprivate clubs derive income from a combination of dues and fees. Additional income for all types of courses is generated by sales of food, beverages, and merchandise; golf lessons and tournaments; rentals or fees for lockers, golf carts, and equipment; and use of other recreational facilities such as swimming pools, tennis courts, bowling alleys, and party rooms.

MEMBERSHIPS AND GREENS FEES

Private Nonprofit Clubs

Although greens fees may be charged for golf at private clubs, this source of revenue is usually not sufficient to cover the cost of golf course operations, and most private club income is derived from membership fees. Full memberships and social memberships are the main categories, although some clubs offer nonresident memberships, and some offer separate memberships for women.

Daily-Fee Courses

Daily-fee golf courses also offer memberships in various categories—annual unlimited play, annual weekday, associate, and senior and junior memberships—to encourage golfers to use their facilities regularly.

With an unlimited play annual membership, a golfer is usually entitled to reserve starting times in addition to unlimited play. The National Golf Foundation reports that the typical annual fee for one adult is about $300; for a couple, $450; for each junior family member (under 21), $50. Weekday annual membership permits golfers to play unlimited rounds Monday through Friday. The cost is usually about 40% less than the cost of an unlimited play membership. Associate membership entitles holders to starting times, but they pay the going greens fee. Dues typically range from $10 to $50. Senior and junior memberships usually entitle golfers who are over 65 or under 18 years of age to unlimited golfing on weekdays. Cost for this type of membership is usually from $100 to $150.[1]

The range of greens fees charged at daily fee courses is extremely wide. Quality of the course, facilities offered, and geographic location are some of the variables that affect cost to play. In the northern part of the country where the playing season is 30 weeks, a typical annual charge is $165 for one adult and $255 for a couple.

Municipal golf courses do not offer memberships as such, but they do offer season passes and reduced fees for local residents and for nonresidents. Greens fees are also usually separated into those for residents and those for nonresidents because the goal of pricing is to offer rates to residents that are lower than comparable courses in the area. Nonresident fees are set to be competitive with comparable courses.

The results of a study conducted by a municipal course in suburban Chicago are shown in Tables 6.1 and 6.2. Rates at 14 municipal golf courses were analyzed to establish a competitive rate structure. Charges shown are typical for the area for 1979.

---

1. Harry C. Eckhoff, *Daily Fee Golf Courses: Pay-as-You-Play Country Clubs,* Information Sheet DF-1 (North Palm Beach, FL: National Golf Foundation, n.d.)

Table 6.1. Season Passes and Reduced Fees — Municipal Courses

Course	Adult Description	Adult Amount	Junior Description	Junior Amount	Senior Description	Senior Amount
A	9 holes 10-play pass, weekdays (Monday-Friday)	$ 23.00	10-play pass, weekdays	$ 20.00	10-play pass, weekdays	$ 20.00
B	18 holes Unlimited resident Limited, weekdays, resident Unlimited, nonresident	$190.00 $125.00 $350.00	Limited weekdays and after 3 pm on weekends	$ 90.00	Limited weekdays and after 3 pm on weekends	$ 60.00
C	Limited, resident, individual Limited, resident, family pass. Entitles $2.50 discount on greens fee	$150.00 $250.00 $ 15.00	Pass entitles juniors (12-17 yrs.) to $2 greens fees before 3 pm weekdays	$ 5.00	Pass entitles seniors to $2 greens fees before 3 pm weekdays	N/C
D	Weekday Unlimited	$175.00 $400.00	Weekday	$125.00	Weekday	$125.00
E	Unlimited Limited	$155.00 $115.00	12-13 year olds 14-15 year olds 16-17 year olds	$ 45.00 $ 65.00 $ 85.00	Weekdays only	$125.00
F	Individual Couple	$300.00 $400.00	N/A		N/A	
G	Unlimited Limited	$145.00 $100.00	Mon.-Fri., after 4 pm Mon., Tues., Thurs., Fri.	$ 70.00 $ 50.00	Weekday only	$ 70.00
H	N/A		N/A		N/A	

Table 6.1. Season Passes and Reduced Fees — Municipal Courses — Continued

Course	Adult Description	Adult Amount	Junior Description	Junior Amount	Senior Description	Senior Amount
I	Reduced greens fee-$2.00 resident	$ 45.00	Reduced greens fee-$1.00 resident	$ 10.00	Reduced greens fees	N/C
	Reduced greens fee-$1.00 nonresident	$ 90.00	Reduced greens fee-$.50 nonresident	$ 10.00		
	Unlimited, resident	$175.00				
	Unlimited, nonresident	$300.00				
J	Unlimited, individual	$130.00	12-16 year olds	$ 40.00	Weekdays and after 2 pm weekends	$ 90.00
	Unlimited, husband/wife	225.00	17-19 year olds	$ 50.00		
K	Unlimited, resident	$275.00	Limited, 5-day, resident	$150.00	Limited, 5-day, resident	$ 90.00
	Unlimited, nonresident	$395.00				
	Limited, 7-day, resident	$210.00				
	Limited, 7-day, nonresident	$345.00				
	Limited, 5-day, resident	$150.00				
L	Unlimited, resident	$175.00	Limited, resident	$ 70.00	Limited, resident	$ 65.00
	Unlimited, nonresident	$260.00	Limited, nonresident	$105.00	Limited, nonresident	$ 95.00
	Limited, resident	$120.00				
	Limited, nonresident	$175.00				
M	Unlimited, resident	$195.00	Limited, weekdays and after 2 pm weekends	$ 70.00	Limited, weekdays and after 1:30 pm weekends	$ 80.00
	Unlimited, nonresident	$215.00				
	Unlimited couple, resident	$325.00				
	Unlimited couple, non-resident	$345.00				
	Limited, weekdays only	$ 90.00				
N	N/A		N/A		N/A	

Table 6.2. Daily Fees — Municipal Courses

Course	Yards	Par	Weekdays 18 Holes	Weekdays 9 Holes	Weekends 18 Holes	Weekends 9 Holes
A	6,541	72	Nonres. $6.00 Resident $5.00	Nonres. $3.75 Resident $3.25	$7.50 after 1 pm $6.00 after 3 pm $4.00	
B	6,800	72	Nonres. $7.00 Resident $5.00	after 4 pm $4.25	$8.50 after 2 pm $6.50 after 4 pm $4.25	after 2 pm $4.25
C	6,340	70	$7.00 after 3 pm $5.00	after 6 pm $2.50	$8.50 after 1 pm $6.50 after 4 pm $4.50	after 6 pm $2.50
D	6,772	72	$6.50 after 3 pm $4.00	$4.00	$9.00 after 1 pm $7.00 after 3 pm $5.00	$5.00 Dawn to 8 am
E	6,200	71	$9.00 after 3:30 $5.00	$4.50	$10.00 after 3:30 $5.00	$5.00
F	6,025	72	$5.75 after 4 pm $4.00	$3.75	$7.50 after 1 pm $6.00 after 4 pm $4.50	
G	6,055	70	$6.50 after 3:30 $4.25	$4.50	$9.00 after 3:30 $5.25	
H	6,400	72	$6.50 after 3 pm $4.00	$4.00	$8.50 after 3 pm $5.25	
I	6,136	69	$7.50 after 3 pm $4.00 Junior $3.50	$4.00 after 3 pm $2.50	$9.00 after 3 pm $5.50 Junior $5.50	
J	6,347	71	$7.50 after 4 pm $5.00		$9.00 after 4 pm $5.50	
K	6,825	72	Non res. $8.50 Resident $6.00	Nonres. $4.75 Resident $3.75	Nonres. $10.00 Resident $7.00 after 3 pm $5.25	Nonres. $5.50 Resident $4.50
L	6,832	72	$6.00	$4.50	$8.00 after 3 pm $5.50	
M	6,394	72	$6.00 after 3 pm $4.50	$4.50	$9.00 after 3 pm $6.50	
N	6,570	72	$7.00 after 4 pm $5.25 (rates reduced $1.00 for residents)	$5.00	$9.00 after 4 pm $6.50	

EXPENSES

In reviewing the present and historical operation of a golf course, the appraiser analyzes expenses in the following categories:

- Operation—salaries, payroll taxes, supplies, maintenance and repairs, equipment reserves, golf association dues, other recreational facilities
- Cost of goods sold—food, beverages, and merchandise
- Administration—manager and staff salaries, payroll taxes, office supplies, insurance, utilities
- Fixed charges—rent, taxes, licenses, interest on debt, legal and accounting fees
- Depreciation and rehabilitation

Maintenance

Costs for golf course maintenance, always one of the largest expense categories, have tripled during the past 20 years, with payroll and related costs almost doubling during the same period (see Figure 6.1 and Table 6.3).

Cost of labor for maintenance, a high expense item, is calculated by man-hours for the various jobs required to keep the golf course in good playing condition. Most 18-hole courses can be well maintained by five crew members, each working 40 hours a week, with fewer hours required during the first and last months of the season.

Equipment used is a consideration in figuring man-hours for most maintenance jobs. Examples of the impact of type of equipment can be seen in the difference in time required to mow fairways with a 5-gang mower compared to a 9-gang Parkmaster and the time involved to water a course manually compared to that expended with a fully automatic irrigation system. With equipment now widely used, the number of man-hours has decreased substantially from that required in the past. A reasonable current estimate of time to mow 18 greens with a triplex mower is four hours. The same mower adjusts to mow fringes so the fringe cut is made at the same time. Greens are normally cut six or seven times a week, so the total man-hours can be calculated based on the length of the golf season.

Figure 6.1. Rise in Golf Course Maintenance Costs. Yearly average costs per hole are represented.

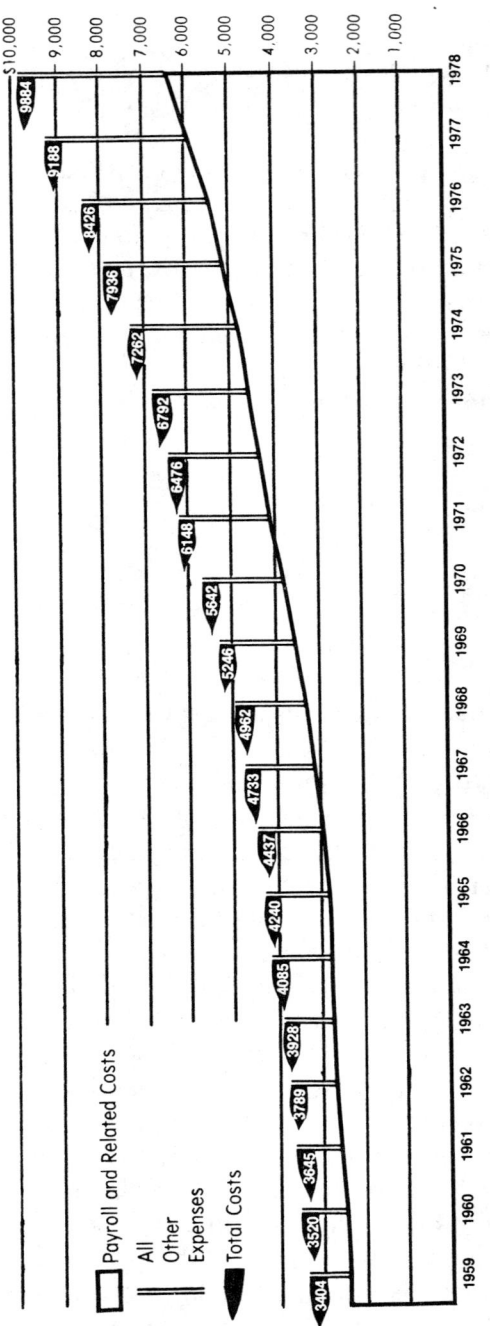

Reprinted with permission of the national accounting firm of Harris, Kerr, Forster & Company.

Table 6.3. Golf Course Maintenance Costs for Country Clubs

	Overall Average	Geographical Divisions			
		East	South	Midwest	Far West
Average cost per hole, 1978					
Payroll	$ 5,449	$ 4,672	$ 6,293	$ 4,886	$ 6,589
Payroll taxes and employee benefits	935	844	934	733	1,193
Course supplies and contracts	1,486	1,306	1,976	1,468	1,573
Repairs to equipment, course buildings, water and drainage system, etc.	987	768	1,089	880	1,324
All other expenses	1,027	816	1,116	788	1,440
Total golf course maintenance	$ 9,884	$ 8,406	$11,408	$ 8,755	$12,119
Add golf shop, caddy, and committee expenses	1,511	1,173	2,145	1,504	1,758
Total golf expenses	$11,395	$ 9,579	$13,553	$10,259	$13,877
Less income from golf fees, golf carts, driving range, etc.	4,327	2,920	6,447	3,095	6,319
Net golf expenses	$ 7,068	$ 6,659	$ 7,106	$ 7,164	$ 7,558
Percentage variations—1978 based on 1977					
Payroll	+ 6.8%	+ 5.0%	+ 8.2%	+ 6.5%	+ 8.2%
Payroll taxes and employee benefits	+12.7	+11.9	+10.4	+ 9.9	+15.4
Course supplies and contracts	+ 7.1	+ 4.6	+ 9.4	+ 8.7	+ 7.9
Repairs to equipment, course buildings, water and drainage system, etc.	+ 8.7	+ 6.2	+ 7.9	+ 9.6	+10.7
All other expenses	+ 7.0	+ 6.3	+ 7.7	+ 5.9	+ 7.5
Total golf course maintenance	+ 7.6%	+ 5.8%	+ 8.5%	+ 7.4%	+ 9.0%
Golf shop, caddy, and committee expenses	+ 8.6	+10.1	+ 7.5	+ 7.7	+ 8.3
Total golf expenses	+ 7.7%	+ 6.4%	+ 8.3%	+ 7.5%	+ 8.9%
Income from golf fees, golf carts, driving range, etc.	+ 6.6	+ 6.7	+ 6.2	+ 6.0	+ 6.8
Net golf expenses	+ 8.4%	+ 6.2%	+10.3%	+ 8.1%	+10.8%

Source: *Clubs in Town and Country 1978* (New York: Harris, Kerr, Forster & Co., 1979), p. 16.

Along with payroll and related expenses, which are commonly 60 to 65% of total expenses, other items in the maintenance budget include:

- Tree planting and landscaping
- Water, depending on source and agreement, such as irrigation water from surface water rights
- New machinery and equipment (unless a capital expense)
- Hand tools and supplies
- Seed, fertilizer, fungicides, topsoil, sand, gravel, peat moss
- Gas, lubricants, electricity
- Equipment repairs and maintenance
- Course reconstruction

The maintenance expense statement must be scrutinized for excessive items that may tend to distort the figures. Such items could include:

- Excess grounds maintenance (usually high-maintenance areas around the clubhouse and other buildings)
- Maintenance of nongolf areas (tennis courts, swimming pools, parking lots, etc.)
- Capital improvements (tree plantings, sand traps, new tees, golf cart paths, bridges, or other construction that is expensed rather than capitalized)
- Fertilization of roughs or trees, or hiring a staff arborist to maintain trees
- Higher-performance maintenance equipment than necessary
- Deferred or advance expenditures (fertilizers or other materials paid for in a period other than that in which they are used)

If variables are not reflected and maintenance of only greens, tees, and fairways is considered, a typical range for maintenance of an 18-hole golf course can be stated. Annual maintenance for a northern course may range from $75,000 to $100,000; for a southern year-round course, the range may be $125,000 to $150,000. These are average figures, and allowance must be made for nonaverage courses such as those with many high-maintenance sand traps, or an abundance of trees to be trimmed and mowed around, or a hilly terrain, or types of turf that are unusually expensive to maintain, or unique climatic conditions (e.g., salt spray, high winds, or lack of water). Obviously the appraiser must carefully analyze the maintenance needs and expenses of the subject golf course and use typical needs and expenses as a guide only.

INCOME AND EXPENSE STATEMENTS

The following statements from representative country clubs, daily-fee courses, and a municipal course are presented for comparative analysis.

COUNTRY CLUB 1

Description

Country Club 1 is located in a suburb of a midwestern city. The club is owned by an employee organization of a large company. The site is approximately 250 acres, most of which has been improved with a regulation 18-hole golf course and clubhouse facility. The course, which was designed and built in the late 1960s, covers roughly 180 acres and has been well maintained.

The clubhouse is in excellent condition, with an attractive brick and stone exterior. The two-story structure contains roughly 33,000 gross square feet of floor area. Facilities within the clubhouse include a 250-seat snack bar, pro shop, men's locker room, women's locker room, cart storage area, club storage rooms, office for club management and staff, two large lounge areas, and two private meeting rooms. There are also two large decks extending off the clubhouse which are used for summer barbecues and dances.

Adjoining the clubhouse are four tennis courts completed in 1978. In addition, a preliminary layout for a 9-hole executive course was begun during 1978.

Country Club 1. Membership (1978)[a]

	Employees		Nonemployees	
	Fee	Number of Members	Fee	Number of Members
Family	$330.00	65	$ 680.00	36
Family (retired)	181.50	23	N/A	N/A
Junior family[b]	N/A	N/A	350.00	8
Individual male	225.00	38	465.00	45
Individual male (retired)	123.75	19	N/A	N/A
Individual female	118.00	10	240.00	12
Individual female (retired)	64.90	4	N/A	N/A
Associate[c]	47.00	9	95.00	49
Associate (retired)	47.00	1	N/A	N/A
Corporate[d]	N/A	N/A	1,500.00	15
Social	5.00	1,015	20.00	293
Ski[e]	——	——	35.00	56
Tennis	——	——	75.00	5

[a] All golf memberships are subject to a $60.00 per quarter minimum charge. No initiation fees are charged.
[b] Junior family memberships apply when neither applicant has reached his 30th birthday.
[c] Associate members have reservation and events restrictions.
[d] Corporate memberships entitle a company to four employees as full golf membership.
[e] Ski and tennis memberships are included in family memberships for employees.

Country Club 1. Statement of Operations and Accumulated Equity

	1st 9 Months 1978	1977	1976	1975
			Year Ended December 31	
Revenue				
Food and beverage sales	$ 305,283	$ 374,409	$ 354,313	$ 291,973
Membership dues	142,939	119,941	108,851	104,524
Golf shop sales	44,377	58,754	51,780	50,230
Green fees	36,018	44,104	44,544	43,196
Driving range and cart rentals	34,119	32,675	29,382	26,893
Locker rent and club storage	9,787	9,741	9,941	9,883
Monthly minimum charges	7,471	16,153		
Other	6,252	11,123	7,216	9,719
Total revenue	$ 586,246	$ 666,900	$ 606,027	$ 536,418
Expenses				
Food and beverage cost of sales	$ 128,729	$ 161,341	$ 148,997	$ 122,870
Golf shop cost of sales	27,044	43,679	37,271	34,545
Salaries and related expenses	250,321	289,453	260,162	219,665
Depreciation and amortization	37,484	49,721	53,292	55,105
Interest	14,156	15,264	11,884	37,079
Property taxes	46,059	57,061	52,996	68,410
Utilities	38,493	39,988	40,309	37,851
Rentals and leased equipment	6,379	6,902	11,504	13,772
Supplies	22,904	44,687	34,402	24,171
Insurance	19,577	22,056	24,366	22,362
Maintenance and repairs	17,855	36,742	37,292	32,598
Security expense	3,685	5,815	5,128	4,900
Club entertainment	5,546	10,955	10,672	12,191
Employee meals	7,223	7,724	7,805	5,296
Advertising	8,659	8,915	4,133	1,947
Uniforms and laundry	10,181	9,774	11,906	8,134
Dishes, glasses and silverware	1,237	11,225	4,418	3,550
Service	5,398	2,709	3,541	3,205
Vending machine purchases	3,112	2,983	2,667	2,459
Postage	3,530	4,552	4,372	1,926
Other	2,179	16,355	9,623	6,407
Total expenses	$ 659,751	$ 847,901	$ 776,740	$ 718,443
Net (loss from operations	$ (73,505)	$ (181,001)	$ (170,713)	$ (182,025)
Gain on sale of land				261,225
Contributions		10,400	76,619	145,000
Net income (loss)	$ (73,505)	$ (170,601)	$ (94,094)	$ 224,200
Accumulated equity, beginning of year	980,403	1,151,004	1,245,098	1,020,898
Accumulated equity, end of year	$ 906,898	$ 980,403	$1,151,004	$1,245,098

COUNTRY CLUB 2

Description

Country Club 2 is located in east central New Jersey. The club was built by a large development-oriented corporation and operated as a private club.

The site is 139 acres, containing an excellently maintained 18-hole golf course, a driving range with several practice greens, four lighted tennis courts, a swimming pool, and a clubhouse.

The 12,000-square-foot clubhouse has 400 men's lockers, 100 women's lockers, large pro shop, card room, steam room, sauna, massage room, a dining room to seat 300 and other luxurious amenities typical of private clubs.

At the time the income information was prepared, the club had 82 full family members at $1,100, 73 individual members at $695, plus some social and corporate memberships.

Country Club 2. Income Statement (Fiscal Year Ended March 31, 1976)

Revenue	
Membership dues	$ 206,915
Restaurant	412,710
Bar	140,756
Cart rentals	71,108
Locker rentals	7,167
Guest fees	30,911
Other	9,114
Total revenue	$ 878,681
Operating expenses	
Restaurant	$ 496,228
Bar	67,215
Cart rentals	35,770
Golf course	147,606
Clubhouse	302,947
Locker rentals	9,688
Total operating expenses	$1,059,454
Net operating gain (loss)	($ 180,773)
Add back depreciation	99,712
Operating loss	($ 81,061)

Country Club 2. Golf Course Operation

Salaries	
Golf pros	$ 16,047
Golf maintenance	64,883
Payroll taxes and benefits	10,490
Vacation pay, salaried employees	3,804
Employee meals	2,400
Course supplies	21,733
Course repairs	10,917
Repairs and maintenance	8,675
Depreciation, golf course equipment	7,889
Special golf course expenses	768
Total golf course operations	$147,606

Country Club 2. Bar

Revenue	
Catering	$ 63,878
Restaurant	76,878
	$ 140,756
Liquor costs	$ 37,372
Bar supplies	5,526
Salaries	17,617
Payroll taxes and benefits	2,290
Vacation pay, salaried employees	1,056
Employee meals	1,200
License and permits	2,154
Total operating costs	$ 67,215
Operating profit	$ 73,541

Country Club 2. Restaurant

Revenue		
Catering		$ 157,880
Restaurant		254,830
		$ 412,710
Food costs		$ 235,969
Salaries		160,299
Payroll taxes and benefits		20,559
Employee meals		6,000
Vacation pay, salaried employees		4,416
Vacation pay, hourly employees		1,912
Laundry		19,608
Depreciation, machinery and equipment		4,326
Depreciation, linen		2,856
Depreciation, kitchen supplies		15,576
Entertainment		7,002
Menus		680
Restaurant supplies		17,025
Total operating costs		$ 496,228
Net operating margin (loss)		($ 83,518)
Add members minimums		—
Operating loss		($ 83,518)

Country Club 2. Cart Rentals

Revenue	$ 71,108
Salaries	$ 11,660
Payroll taxes and benefits	1,925
Depreciation	17,695
Repairs and maintenance	4,490
Total operating costs	$ 35,770
Operating profit	$ 35,338

Country Club 2. Clubhouse Operations

Salaries
- Manager — $ 18,371
- Clerical and bookkeeping — 14,980
- Maintenance — 12,702
- Tennis — —
- Valets — —
- Lifeguards — 1,961
- Instructors — —

Payroll taxes and benefits	6,294
Vacation pay	2,172
Employee meals	3,000
Garbage collection	2,840
Pool supplies	802
Stationery, printing, office	8,265
Telephone	8,380
Heat, light, power	60,634
Depreciation, building	39,791
Depreciation, furniture	7,547
Real estate taxes	46,987
Amortized, preopening expenses	4,032
Miscellaneous expenses	2,255
Advertising	1,770
Clubhouse supplies	—
Building maintenance	6,992
Game room supplies	356
Travel	1,503
Repairs and maintenance	14,730
Bookkeeping services	4,400
Consulting services	12,400
Insurance	16,800
Outside security	1,008
Equipment rental expense	683
Pool maintenance	1,292
Total clubhouse operations	$302,947

Country Club 2. Locker Room Operation

Revenue	$ 7,167
Salaries	$ 8,849
Payroll taxes and benefits	839
Towel rental (pool and golf)	--
Total operating expenses	$ 9,688
Operating profit (loss)	$(2,521)

Country Club 2.   Pro Forma Cash Flow Profit Based on 1975 Actual and 1976 Budget

	1976	1977
Income		
Restaurant	$490,000	
Less labor and fringe benefits (35%)	$171,500	
Cost of goods (45%)	220,000	
Other direct expense	37,500	
Profit to club	$ 61,000	$ 61,000
Bar	$155,000	
Less labor and fringe benefits	20,500	
Cost of goods	40,000	
Other direct expense	4,500	
Profit to club	$ 90,000	$ 90,000
Membership dues	$230,000	$275,000
Golf cart rentals	80,000	100,000
Guest fees	30,000	37,000
Pro shop income	75,000	90,000
Driving range income	5,000	7,000
Subtotal	$420,000	$509,000
Less cost of goods—pro shop	56,000	67,500
Profit to club	$364,000	$441,500
Total income (gross profit)	$515,000	$592,500
Expenses		
Golf course	$117,000	$117,000
Golf carts	24,000	30,000
Clubhouse	232,500	207,500
Golf pro salary (plus lessons)	20,000	20,000
	$393,500	$374,500
Cash flow profit[a]	$121,500	$218,000

[a] Cash flow profit is net profit plus depreciation and interest—the cash left to pay amortization and profit.

DAILY-FEE COURSE 1

Description

This course is located in southeastern Florida in a large metropolitan area. This course is 18 holes, all irrigated, 6,970 yards, par 72, on 140 acres. There is a 4,500-square-foot clubhouse valued at $175,000 where liquor and meals are served. The restaurant and lounge are leased at 7½% of gross sales plus certain prorated expenses. The pro shop and driving range were leased out for nine months of 1978 at 20% of sales and certain prorated expenses.

Daily-Fee Course 1. Unaudited Statement of Income and Retained Earnings

	1978	1977	1976	1975
Income				
Green fees and cart rental	$495,452	$489,625	$458,849	$457,998
Membership dues	46,190	26,730	28,381	31,067
Pro shop sales	12,758	104,729	145,725	193,860
Driving range income	7,626	36,552	33,225	23,690
Club rental	4,343	3,597	3,924	3,793
Restaurant sales	8,087	51,840	54,180	115,121
Lounge sales	7,777	42,902	46,751	91,017
Entertainment income	—	—	—	13,242
Golf lessons	662	2,720	1,456	15,566
Income from leased operations	27,506	—	—	—
Other income	20,032	18,443	13,578	9,483
Total income	$630,433	$777,138	$786,069	$954,837
Operating expenses	498,369	691,854	669,203	828,689
Operating income	$132,064	$ 85,284	$116,866	$126,148
Other charges				
Interest expense	$106,712	$ 57,696	$ 47,178	$ 43,072
Bonuses	10,400	18,000	25,550	31,428
Professional services	6,688	1,350	3,500	6,451
Officer's life insurance	6,475	4,276	3,784	3,253
Directors expenses	1,506	1,963	1,029	9,897
Total other charges	$131,781	$ 83,285	$ 81,041	$ 94,101
Income before income taxes[a]	$ 283	$ 1,999	$ 35,825	$ 32,047
State income taxes	—	64	—	—
Income before extraordinary item[a]	$ 283	$ 1,935	$ 35,825	$ 32,047
Nonrecurring interest expense	9,376	—	—	—
Net income (loss)[a]	$ (9,093)	$ 1,935	$ 35,825	$ 32,047
Less distributions	—	(39,735)	—	(52,806)
Retained earnings (deficit) beginning of year	(1,975)	35,825	-0-	20,759
Retained earnings (deficit) end of year	$ (11,068)	$ (1,975)	$ 35,825	$ -0-

[a] Per share $.01 in 1978; $.04 in 1977; $.69 in 1976 and $.62 in 1975.

Daily-Fee Course 1. Unaudited Schedule of Operating Expenses

	1978	1977	1976	1975
Payroll, administrative	$ 32,000	$ 24,000	$ 24,000	$ 20,000
Payroll, golf course	81,897	78,876	66,360	66,287
Payroll, golf service	9,115	10,612	6,503	27,971
Payroll, golf pro	4,296	21,589	24,301	38,828
Payroll, pro shop	22,300	33,037	22,429	22,352
Payroll, restaurant and lounge	4,100	41,509	39,467	69,699
Pro shop merchandise purchases	8,326	98,517	116,796	152,112
Restaurant purchases	5,301	24,550	28,830	55,068
Lounge purchases	4,695	18,079	18,218	28,594
Electric cart expense	47,404	29,222	16,065	15,473
Gas and oil	4,131	4,834	4,234	5,504
Fertilizer	15,200	17,754	16,103	5,525
Chemicals	14,021	12,582	6,509	28,448
Laundry	–	–	–	2,111
Parts and repairs	20,198	18,343	20,120	19,450
Golf course expense	16,502	23,818	19,291	23,653
Pro shop expense	127	449	3,148	912
Restaurant and lounge expense	2,907	15,812	11,586	18,003
Advertising and promotion	38,830	35,773	33,256	28,428
Amortization	4,766	–	–	250
Auto expense	3,809	3,849	3,878	4,863
Clubhouse expense	2,624	2,269	4,961	1,824
Commissions	1,706	2,505	3,585	8,179
Depreciation	47,424	46,228	45,826	39,630
Dues and subscriptions	844	274	510	600
Insurance	23,798	21,694	20,310	17,621
Live entertainment	–	–	–	16,802
Professional services	6,141	6,631	6,610	5,970
Office expense	2,527	3,927	4,362	5,836
Other expense	2,041	1,247	1,111	1,281
Payroll taxes	12,615	14,450	13,029	14,826
Postage	1,606	1,821	2,160	1,694
Property taxes	15,003	14,415	14,278	9,254
Rent	12,432	37,296	37,296	37,296
Taxes and licenses	1,552	3,242	5,326	5,160
Telephone	3,422	3,520	3,085	3,357
Travel and entertainment	3,234	2,072	1,363	1,088
Utilities, clubhouse	11,753	17,496	13,397	14,643
Utilites, golf course	9,722	10,562	10,900	10,097
	$498,369	$691,854	$669,203	$828,689

DAILY-FEE COURSE 2

Description

This course is located in northwestern Massachusetts. It is 6,000 yards, par 72, on 125 acres of rolling and wooded land. There are 13 other golf courses in the market area (population: 130,000). The clubhouse is 7,000 square feet and is valued at $175,000. Liquor and meals are served.

Wages appear high in relation to size of facility and sales. The $11,000 salary for the pro and $19,500 manager's salary may have upset the balance. The total of wages and payroll taxes is $76,750 and probably should be around $55,000, which would increase profits to $63,000.

Daily-Fee Course 2. Financial Report for 1978

Income

Membership	$ 18,110	
Daily fees	86,000	
Cart rentals	26,700	
Club storage and repairs	1,000	
Lessons	1,532	
Handicaps, lockers, miscellaneous	400	
Clubhouse (restaurant, bar)	39,200	
Golf shop merchandise	33,900	
	$206,842	$206,842
Purchases (equalizing inventory)		
Clubhouse	$ 17,000	
Golf shop	21,200	
	$ 38,200	$ 38,200
		$168,642

Expenses (not including interest, depreciation and nonrecurring expenses)

Advertising and promotion	$ 1,579	
Dues and subscriptions	318	
Employees transportation	747	
Gas and oil	2,600	
Legal and audit	1,252	
Laundry	800	
Maintenance	1,200	
Office wages (secretary)	2,250	
Officer (manager-superintendent)	19,500	
Golf pro	11,000	
Course maintenance wages	14,622	
Clubhouse and golf shop	21,378	
Insurance	7,300	
Repairs	3,450	
Supplies	5,700	
Payroll taxes	8,000	
Real estate taxes	15,880	
Miscellaneous taxes	975	
Liquor license tax	6,600	
Bank service charge	400	
Miscellaneous	100	
	$126,651	$126,651
Net		$ 41,991

DAILY-FEE COURSE 3

Description

This course is located in Maryland. It is 18 holes, 7,003 yards, par 72, on approximately 200 acres of land. The course is wooded and irrigated. The clubhouse is approximately 5,000 square feet, and there is a large swimming pool.

Income from pro shop and driving range is given to the pro. Cost of goods for food and bar is higher than normal. Storm damage and supervision are high, due to some unusual circumstances.

Daily-Fee Course 3. Statement of Income

	1976	1975
Income		
Operating income, golf course	$82,608	$77,451
Operating income, swimming pool	14,042	15,972
Operating (loss), clubhouse	(7,300)	(10,617)
Interest income	2,602	2,300
Other income	200	--
Total income	$92,152	$85,106
Administrative expenses		
Amortization	$ --	$ 65
Auto expense	--	800
Depreciation of paving costs	67	33
Dues and subscriptions	249	165
Storm damages	5,127	1,500
Insurance	5,338	4,175
Interest	19,133	19,623
Legal and accounting	6,056	6,154
Office supplies and expense	595	1,761
Salaries	12,420	9,843
Supervision	6,000	4,200
Payroll taxes	995	669
Real estate taxes	14,323	15,433
Other taxes	995	1,003
Telephone	1,358	1,135
Total administrative expenses	$72,656	$66,559
Income before income taxes	$19,496	$18,547
Provision for income taxes	--	--
Net income	$19,496	$18,547

Daily-Fee Course 3. Schedule of Golf Courses Operating Income and Expenses

	1976	1975
Income		
Dues and initiation fees	$ 36,609	$ 41,540
Green fees, B members	8,303	9,643
Green fees, F members and guests	82,903	86,587
Electric carts	50,105	50,571
Lockers	615	739
Total income	$178,535	$189,080
Operating expenses		
Maintenance	$ 10,042	$ 19,507
Golf course fuel and oil	2,861	3,369
Utilities	3,875	3,919
Salaries	32,666	38,508
Pro commissions	9,880	9,538
Commissions for electric carts	23,688	23,969
Cash shortages	84	40
Payroll taxes	2,621	2,628
Depreciation	10,126	9,363
Miscellaneous	84	788
Total operating expenses	$ 95,927	$111,629
Operating income golf course	$ 82,608	$ 77,451

Daily-Fee Course 3. Schedule of Swimming Pool Operating Income and Expenses

	1976	1975
Income		
Apartment fees and guest fees	$ 9,071	$ 9,234
Dues and initiation fees	24,866	24,122
Total income	$33,937	$33,356
Operating expenses		
Payroll taxes	$ 669	$ 615
Salaries	8,341	8,982
Pool supplies and maintenance	7,275	4,552
Depreciation	3,610	3,235
Total operating expenses	$19,895	$17,384
Operating income, swimming pool	$14,042	$15,972

Daily-Fee Course 3. Schedule of Clubhouse Operation

	1976		1975	
Sales, food and miscellaneous	$35,231		$34,855	
Less cost of sales	20,862		20,101	
Gross profit	$14,369		$14,754	
Percentage of sales		40.8%		42.3%
Sales, beer	$28,283		$27,245	
Less cost of sales	11,801		11,464	
Gross profit	$16,482		$15,781	
Percentage of sales		58.3%		57.9%
Sales, liquor	$18,672		$20,397	
Less cost of sales	5,166		7,169	
Gross profit	$13,506		$13,228	
Percentage of sales		72.3%		64.9%
Miscellaneous income	$ 1,844		$ 1,656	
Total clubhouse gross income	$46,201		$45,419	
Expenses				
Salaries	$26,352		$30,204	
Taxes and licenses	960		960	
Trash removal	805		780	
Cash shortages	524		623	
Repairs and maintenance	2,146		1,531	
Utilities	11,625		11,756	
Payroll taxes	2,097		2,060	
Miscellaneous	909		-0-	
Band	258		781	
Supplies	3,531		2,583	
Depreciation	4,294		4,758	
Total expenses	$53,501		$56,036	
Operating (loss)	$ (7,300)		$(10,617)	

DAILY-FEE COURSE 4

Description

This course is located in western North Carolina in a town of less than 3,000 population, but there are many small towns within the market area. The course is 18 holes, 6,575 yards, par 72, on approximately 140 acres of rolling land. The greens and tees are watered; fairways are not. The clubhouse is approximately 5,000 square feet on ground floor and is two stories high. The course owns 50 carts and stores 20 privately owned golf carts.

This course was appraised in 1977 for $725,000.

Daily-Fee Course 4. Statement of Income, Expense and Retained Earnings (1976)

Income

Membership fees, concession sales, pro shop sales and tournament fees	$206,014.97	
Less state sales tax included in sales	4,369.01	$201,645.96

Cost of sales

Inventory, January 1, 1976	$ 4,748.28	
Pro shop and concession purchases	32,636.26	
Subtotal	37,384.54	
Less inventory December 31, 1976	5,312.25	
Cost of merchandise sold	$ 32,072.29	
Depreciation	17,955.61	
Gasoline and oil	3,708.07	
Golf course supplies and fertilizer	10,422.00	
Concession supplies	158.21	
Insurance	9,710.03	
Property taxes	2,408.67	
Tournament expense and banquet	1,340.82	
Trophies	400.13	
Repairs	11,526.04	
Truck expense	841.01	
Salaries	40,062.41	
Payroll taxes	2,908.01	
Cost of sales		133,513.30
Gross profit		$ 68,132.66

(Continued)

Daily-Fee Course 4. Statement of Income—Continued

Expenses

Administrative salaries	$ 25,361.25	
Advertising	240.00	
Donations	108.50	
Dues and subscriptions	491.00	
Freight	100.42	
Heat, lights, and water	2,464.75	
Interest	4,543.75	
Laundry and linen	215.07	
Miscellaneous	595.30	
Office supplies and postage	559.00	
Payroll taxes	1,840.90	
Professional fees	1,228.00	
Medical expense reimbursement plan	635.80	
Telephone	849.08	
Other business taxes	356.48	
Travel expense	70.95	39,660.25
Net operating profit income before taxes		$ 28,472.41
Less federal income tax		4,611.28
Operating income		$ 23,861.13

DAILY-FEE COURSE 5

Description

This course is located in a suburb of a Michigan industrial city with a metropolitan population of around 120,000. The course is 18 hole, 6,312 yards, par 72, on 142 acres of land. It has a 101-foot x 47-foot clubhouse with living quarters above. The course is heavily wooded, fully irrigated, mostly located within a flood plain.

This course was sold in 1978 for $675,000.

Daily-Fee Course 5. Profit and Loss Statement (1977)

	Year to Date	%
Income		
Sales		
Green fees	$134,732.07	
Retail	37,982.12	
Club rental	606.95	
Cart rental	32,390.88	
Food	22,229.71	
Take out	4,519.41	
Beer and wine	25,506.23	
Liquor	9,631.51	
C.O.A.D.	5,613.66	
Other	(63.18)	
Total sales	$273,139.36	100.0
Cost of sales		
Beginning inventory	$ 16,004.70	5.9
Purchases	28,651.07	10.5
Purchases, Food	15,441.07	5.7
Purchases, Bar	19,202.98	7.0
Own use	(594.75)	(.2)
Ending inventory	(12,834.56)	(4.7)
Total cost of sales	$ 65,870.51	24.1
Gross profit	$207,268.85	75.9

(Continued)

Daily-Fee Course 5. Profit and Loss Statement—Continued

	Year to Date	%
General and Admin. Expense		
Salaries and wages	$ 35,348.64	12.9
Advertising	1,128.31	.4
Auto and truck expense	2,676.12	1.0
Cleaning	372.01	.3
Commissions	.00	.0
Depreciation	10,968.98	4.0
Dues and subscriptions	438.00	.2
Freight	18.65	.0
Heat, power and light	5,657.71	2.1
Insurance	7,148.98	2.6
Interest	21,326.87	7.8
Legal and accounting	1,079.00	.4
Licenses and permits	851.00	.3
Miscellaneous expense	30.00	.0
Equipment rental	$ 18,364.78	6.7
Repair and maintenance	9,949.96	3.6
Supplies	5,121.30	1.9
Taxes		
Sales	3,811.35	1.4
FICA	2,065.47	.8
Real estate	20,683.20	7.6
Other	4,189.52	1.5
Federal unemployment	224.18	.1
State unemployment	2,219.40	.8
Telephone and telegraph	1,933.21	.7
Travel and entertainment	.00	.0
Total	$156,106.64	57.2
Net profit or loss	$ 51,162.21	18.7

DAILY-FEE COURSE 6

Description

This course is located in a suburb of Detroit, Michigan. This course is 18 hole, 6,132 yards, par 72, on 132 acres of land. It has a 7,150-square-foot clubhouse serving liquor and meals. The course is fully irrigated.

In 1977 more than 49,000 rounds of golf were played on the course. A number of these rounds were 9 holes; if all the rounds had been 18 holes, it would have amounted to approximately 42,000 18-hole rounds.

The total income of $505,000 breaks down as:

Green fees	$245,000
Cart rentals	$ 41,000
Driving range and rentals	$ 16,000
Restaurant	$101,000
Bar	$ 76,000
Pro shop	$ 26,000

Some tree plantings and sand trap construction expense was not capitalized. Almost no sales effort occurred in the pro shop or on the driving range.

This club was sold in 1978 for $950,000.

Daily-Fee Course 6. Income & Expense Statement as of October 31, 1977

Total revenue		$505,027.18
Direct costs		
Wages	$129,108.70	
Payroll taxes	13,460.19	
Fuel, golf course	3,009.99	
Maintenance and repairs	27,297.27	
Sales tax	7,392.85	
Cost of sales	94,174.95	
Depreciation	22,634.24	
Supplies	7,653.61	
Total direct costs		304,731.80
Gross profit		$200,295.38
Less operating expenses		
Advertising	$ 2,903.76	
Auto expenses	485.12	
Business promotion	1,539.78	
Cash over or short	258.03	
Contributions	565.00	
Depreciation	6,275.22	
Directors fees	350.00	
Electricity	11,704.62	
Heating fuel	3,075.30	
Insurance		
General	13,936.17	
Group	4,604.92	
Officers life	1.67	
Workers compensation	4,128.00	
Interest	1,456.32	
Laundry	1,545.40	
License and permits	834.70	
Maintenance, clubhouse	9,541.53	
Membership dues	508.00	
Professional services	4,093.00	

(Continued)

Daily-Fee Course 6. Income Statement — Continued

Repair and maintenance	2,722.10	
Salaries, officers	36,462.04	
Supplies		
General	1,304.22	
Office	1,396.08	
Pro shop	1.46	
Taxes		
General	10.00	
Payroll	2,020.61	
Property	13,912.80	
State corporation	5,877.00	
Telephone	3,785.79	
Trash removal	900.60	
Travel expenses	2,529.77	
Utilities	198.42	
Total operating expenses		138,927.43
Net profit or loss on operations		$ 61,367.95

Other income

Lease income	2,649.60	
Gain on sale of asset	590.90	
Total other income		3,240.50
Net profit before federal income taxes		$ 64,608.45
Less federal income tax		16,019.33
Net profit		$ 48,589.12

Daily-Fee Course 6. Statement of Retained Earnings as of October 31, 1977

Balance at November 1, 1976	$191,553.09
Less dividend paid	(25,856.00)
Plus profit for the fiscal year	48,589.12
	$214,286.21

MUNICIPAL COURSE 1

Description

This course, which was opened for play in 1979, is located in a suburb of Chicago. It is owned and operated by the local park district. The course is 5,045 yards on 90 acres. Water comes into play on most of the 18 holes because of the dual land use—flood water retention and golf.

There is a two-story clubhouse (3,350 square feet on ground level, and 3,600 square feet on the upper level) that includes men's and women's locker rooms, a snack bar, dining room, lounge, banquet facility for 150 to 175 people, pro shop, and maintenance and storage facilities. The clubhouse cost $625,000. Because the course has only begun operation, a budget is presented in lieu of income/expense statements.

Municipal Course 1. Schedule of Daily Fees

	Weekdays		Saturdays-Sundays-Holidays	
	Resident with I.D.	Nonresident and Resident without I.D.	Resident with I.D.	Nonresident and Resident without I.D.
18 holes	$6.00	$8.00	$8.00	$10.00
9 holes	4.00	5.00	5.00	6.00

Note: Seniors (65 and older) will be allowed a $.50 discount for each 9 holes during weekday play prior to 3:30 p.m.

Season passes	Unlimited[a]	Limited[b]
Resident	$275.00	$200.00
Non-Resident	400.00	300.00
Resident, Senior Citizen (65 and older)		150.00
Non-Resident, Senior Citizen (65 and older)		250.00
Resident Youth (17 and under)		150.00

Golf cart fees: pull carts, $1.50, gas carts, 18 holes, $12.00; 9 holes, $7.00

---

[a] Play on any day and time that the course is open to the public.
[b] Play prior to 3:30 pm on any weekday that the course is open to the public.

Municipal Course 1. Budget

	Food Services				Golf Program	Golf Prog. & Food Serv. Unallocated	Maint.	Total	% of Total
	Rest.	Banq.	Snack Bar	Unallocated	Subtotal				
Operating Revenues									
Room rental		$ 1,000			$ 1,000				$ 1,000	—
Food sales	$ 86,300	51,000	$10,300		147,600				147,600	27
Liquor sales	79,700	35,000	8,400		123,100				123,100	23
Banq. serv. & gratuity		15,500			15,500				15,500	3
Greens fees						$137,500			137,500	25
Cart rental						43,000			43,000	8
Cross country ski-equip. rental							3,000		3,000	1
Pro shop sales						7,200			7,200	13
Summary										
Total revenue	$166,000	$102,500	$18,700		$287,200	$255,500			$542,700	100
Less Cost of Goods										
Mech. purchases						52,000			52,000	35
Food purchases	36,300	20,400	4,100		60,800				60,800	41
Liquor purchases	22,300	9,800	2,400		34,500				34,500	24
Subtotal	$ 58,600	$ 30,200	$ 6,500		$ 95,300	$ 52,000			$147,300	100
Gross profit from sales	$107,400	$ 72,300	$12,200		$191,900	$203,500			$395,400	
Operating Expenses										
Salaries & Wages										
Bus. & rev. fac. mgr.							$ 8,800		$ 8,800	2
Asst. supt. of parks								$ 20,500	20,500	5
Clerical, part time							$ 23,000		23,000	5
Custodian, full time								9,600	9,600	2
Custodian, part time								2,500	2,500	—
Maint. labor—full time								20,100	20,100	5

Municipal Course 1. Budget—Continued

		Food Services				Golf Program	Golf Prog. & Food Serv. Unallocated	Maint.	Total	% of Total
	Rest.	Banq.	Snack Bar	Unallocated	Subtotal					

Operating Expenses
Salaries & Wages—Cont.

	Rest.	Banq.	Snack Bar	Unallocated	Subtotal	Golf Program	Golf Prog. & Food Serv. Unallocated	Maint.	Total	% of Total
Maint. labor—part time								$ 15,900	$ 15,900	4
Maint. labor—overtime								1,400	1,400	—
Maint. area supv.								15,000	15,000	3
Concession attendants			$ 6,100		$ 6,100				6,100	1
Facility supv.	$ 22,900	$ 1,300		$19,300	20,600	$ 17,200			37,800	9
Cooks	11,200	4,700			27,600				27,600	6
Bartenders	10,900	2,600			13,800				13,800	3
Waitresses		11,600			22,500				22,500	5
Diswashers & set up	6,700	8,100			14,800				14,800	3
Starters, rangers & cart attendants						8,500			8,500	2
Subtotal	$ 51,700	$ 28,300	$ 6,100	$19,300	$105,400	$ 48,700	$ 8,800	$ 85,000	$247,900	59

Insurance

Group health				800	800	800		3,200	4,800	1
Fire							400	200	600	—
Business interruption							1,000		1,000	—
Dram shop				1,300	1,300				1,300	—
Subtotal				$ 2,100	$ 2,100	$ 800	$ 1,400	$ 3,400	$ 7,700	1

Commodities

Dining rm./lnge/ktchn. supplies				2,200	2,200				2,200	—
Dish room chemicals				3,000	3,000				3,000	—
Janitorial supplies								1,000	1,000	—

Municipal Course 1. Budget—Continued

	Food Service					Golf Program	Golf Prog. & Food Serv. Unallocated	Maint.	Total	% of Total
	Rest.	Banq.	Snack Bar	Unallocated	Subtotal					
Commodities—Cont.										
Paper Supplies	$ 1,300	$ 200	$ 1,600		$ 3,100				3,100	—
Landscape supplies								$ 30,200	$ 30,200	7
Lumber								400	400	—
Small tools								2,000	2,000	—
Structural, shp. mtl. & fixtures								1,800	1,800	—
Gas, oil & antifreeze						$ 700		2,700	3,400	—
Electrical supplies								500	500	—
Paints & solvents								200	200	—
Parts & ftgs., motor veh.								1,200	1,200	—
Parts & ftgs., mowing eqp.								2,000	2,000	—
Parts & ftgs., plumb. & htg.								300	300	—
Commodities, NEC	200	100	100		400	200		500	1,100	—
Subtotal	$ 1,500	$ 300	$ 1,700	$ 5,200	$ 8,700	$ 900		$ 42,800	$ 52,400	13
Contractual Services										
Equipment rental		300	600		900				900	—
Uniform rental								400	400	—
Printing & binding				300	300		2,000		2,300	—
Telephone				700	700	1,200		500	2,400	—
Water								1,000	1,000	—
Gas heat								2,900	2,900	—
Electric	300					18,000		6,700	24,700	6
Prof. serv., other than leg.								300	300	—
Advertising	800	1,300		100	2,200	500			2,700	—
Association dues				100	100	200		100	400	—

Municipal Course 1. Budget—Continued

	Food Service					Golf Program	Golf Prog. & Food Serv. Unallocated	Maint.	Total	% of Total
	Rest.	Banq.	Snack Bar	Unallocated	Subtotal					
Contractual Services—Cont.										
Program services		$ 400			$ 400				$ 400	—
Linen service	$ 900	1,800	$ 300		3,000				3,000	—
Bank serv. chg., credit cards	1,500				1,500				1,500	—
Contractual serv., NEC	700	500	100		1,300	300		300	1,900	—
Subtotal	$ 4,200	$ 4,300	$ 1,100	$800	$ 10,400	$ 2,200	$ 20,000	$ 12,200	$ 44,800	11
Maintenance & Repair										
Building, maint. & repair	300	200	100		600				600	—
Paving, maint. & repair								800	800	—
Fencing, Maint. & repair								600	600	—
Mach. & mech. eqp., maint. & repair	300	200	100		600			900	1,500	—
Vehicle, maint. & repair								300	300	—
Irrigation sys., maint. & repair								3,000	3,000	—
Well & pump, maint. repair								1,000	1,000	—
Subtotal	$ 600	$ 400	$ 200		$ 1,200	$ 600		$ 6,600	$ 7,800	2
Other Expenses										
Travel & personnel exp.				600	600	600		600	1,800	—

Municipal Course 1. Budget—Continued

		Food Services				Golf Program	Golf Prog. & Food Serv. Unallocated	Maint.	Total	% of Total
	Rest.	Banq.	Snack Bar	Unallocated	Subtotal					
Other Expenses—Cont.										
Promotional exp.				$ 500	$ 500				$ 500	—
Interest expense		$ 18,200			18,200				18,200	4
Depreciation exp.							$ 17,500	5,000	22,500	5
Subtotal		$ 18,200		$ 1,100	$ 19,300	$ 600	$ 17,500	$ 5,600	$ 43,000	10
Total operating expenses	$ 58,000	$ 51,500	$ 9,100	$28,500	$147,100	$ 53,200	$ 47,700	$155,600	$403,600	100
Nonoperating Expenditures										
Capital										
Land Improvements								$ 5,000	$ 5,000	15
Food service eqp.	$ 700		$ 4,000	$ 300	$ 5,000				5,000	15
Motor vehicles								15,200	15,200	46
Mach., imp. & major tools				2,000	2,000				2,000	6
Office furn. & eqp.				2,500	2,500				2,500	7
Grounds fixtures								2,000	2,000	6
Capital expenditures, NEC			400		400				400	1
Subtotal	$ 700		$ 4,000	$ 4,800	$ 9,900			$ 22,200	$ 32,100	97
Other										
Contracts payable				1,000	1,000				1,000	3
Subtotal				$ 1,000	$ 1,000				$ 1,000	
Total nonoperating expenditures	$ 700		$ 1,400	$ 4,000	$ 4,800	$ 10,900		$ 22,200	$ 33,100	100
Summary										
Gross profit from sales	107,400	72,300	12,200	—	191,900	203,500	—		395,400	
Less operating expenses	58,000	51,500	9,100	28,500	147,100	53,200	47,700	155,600	403,600	
Net income	$ 49,400	$ 20,800	$ 3,100	$(28,500)	$ 44,800	$150,300	$ (47,700)	$(155,600)	$ (8,200)	

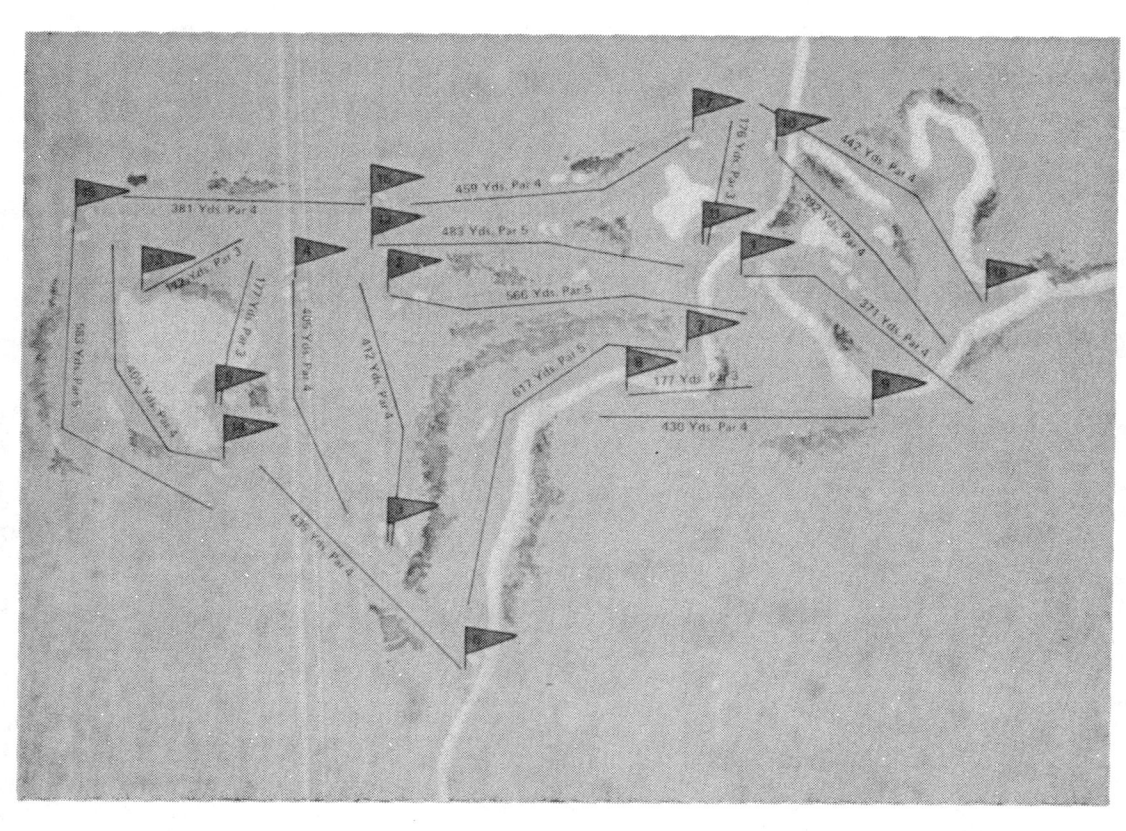

7

Valuation Procedures

The first step in the appraisal process for any property is definition of the problem. Of the factors involved in this definition, the most critical in the appraisal of golf courses is to state the objective of the appraisal so that the value to be estimated can be identified. The objective of a golf course appraisal may be for sale transaction, merger or stock transaction, lease arrangement, feasibility, financing, insurance, ad valorem taxation, or condemnation. Depending on the objective stated, the value sought may be value in exchange or value in use, with specific terms applied, such as *assessed value, going concern value, insurable value, liquidation value, rental value,* or *leasehold value.*

Value in exchange (market value) reflects the actions of buyers, sellers, and investors in the market. The most widely accepted definitions of *market value* are:

> The highest price in terms of money that a property would bring in a competitive and open market under all conditions requisite to a fair sale, the buyer and seller each acting prudently and knowledgeably, and assuming the price is not affected by undue stimulus.

> The price at which a willing seller would sell and a willing buyer would buy, neither being under abnormal pressure.

The price that can be expected if a reasonable time is allowed to find a purchaser and if both seller and prospective buyer are fully informed.

Value in use is the value of a property for a specific use or to a specific user, reflecting the extent to which the property contributes to the utility or profitability of the enterprise of which it is a part. Value in use may or may not represent market value.

The definition of value sought is important at the outset of a golf course appraisal because it will greatly affect the weight given in the assignment to the market data approach, the cost approach, or the income approach. The other primary factor in the use of one or more of the approaches is the type of golf course being appraised—that is, private nonprofit, municipal, or daily-fee.

APPROACHES TO VALUE

As for all real property, the traditional three approaches to value can be applied to a golf course. However, one approach may be more applicable than the others to the type of course being appraised.

If sufficient sales of comparable golf courses are available, the market data (direct sales comparison) approach is used to achieve an estimate of value for any of the three types of golf courses. In the absence of such market data, one of the other two approaches is more appropriate.

Because private nonprofit and municipal courses are not sold so often as daily-fee courses, data may be insufficient for use of the market data approach. Because these types of courses usually do not generate sufficient income for return on investment, application of the income approach is also often precluded. In these situations, if the objective of the appraisal is a sale, use of the cost approach is indicated. The resultant value estimate from the cost approach, applied to private nonprofit and municipal courses, is seldom market value; it is more often value in use. If the objective of the appraisal of a private or municipal course is for other than sale—for example, for a lease arrangement—use of the income approach is indicated.

Because daily fee courses are primarily business ventures, the income approach is applicable. However, this type of course is the one most often sold, so adequate market data would be more likely to exist than for private or municipal courses, making the market data approach also applicable.

Market Data (Direct Sales Comparison) Approach

The market data approach is based on a comparison between the sale prices of similar properties and the property being appraised. For valuing a golf course, *similar properties* are to be those that have been sold for continued use as golf courses, not for future subdivision potential.

The steps in the market data approach are:

1. Seek similar properties for which pertinent sales, listings, offerings, and/or rental data are available.
2. Ascertain the conditions of the sale, including the price, motivating forces, and its bona fide nature.
3. Analyze each of the comparable properties' important attributes in relation to the corresponding attributes of the property being appraised under the general divisions of time, location, physical characteristics, and terms of sale.
4. Consider and adjust for the dissimilarities in the characteristics disclosed in Step 3, in terms of their probable effect on sales prices.
5. Formulate, in the light of the comparisons made, an opinion of the relative value of the property being appraised.

To estimate the degree of comparability between two golf courses, many judgment decisions are required. Although arm's-length sales of golf courses are more common now than they were in the past, thus increasing the amount of available data and strengthening the practicality of using the market data approach, some problems still might arise in its application.

Among the basic requirements for usable comparable sales is that they are recent. Timeliness is relative—what is recent for the sale of a golf course would not be recent for the sale of, say, a single family residence—but since the number of golf course sales is limited, finding reasonably recent comparables may prove problematic. Golf course sales as old as several years may have to be included in the comparison, with adjustment made for time. In addition, the geographic area from which comparables are drawn is necessarily wider than it would be for more commonly sold properties.

Prices received for golf courses are strongly related to terms of sale. Golf courses are often sold with a 20 to 30% down payment, with the seller providing 20-year terms at around 8% interest (as of this writing). Where more generous terms are extended, a higher price may be realized; conversely, where lower or no terms are provided, a lower price may be obtained.

It is always important to find out why a course was sold. A government agency may purchase through condemnation to preserve a greenbelt and pay far in excess of the value attributed to a golf facility. A developer may purchase for land value only. A private club may use some formula for purchase based on anticipated dues, income, and membership stock sales. Some sales are made at high figures due to misinformed purchasers using poor judgment, and some at low figures resulting from financial problems or bankruptcy.

The fact that the designers of golf courses consciously attempt to make each golf course unique makes the comparison of physical characteristics of land and improvements difficult. The many adjustments that must be made for differences between the golf course being appraised and comparables means that many subjective decisions are implicit in the application of the market data approach. Any common factor that is used, such as price per acre or price per hole, can be only a rough estimate because of the great diversity in golf course improvements.

The Cost Approach

The cost approach is based on adding an estimate of the depreciated reproduction cost of the land improvements and buildings to an estimated value of the land.

In estimating the value of golf course land, the appraiser decides on one of two methods: (1) the land is valued by comparison to other parcels that are available for *an alternative highest and best use* or (2) the land is valued by comparison to other parcels that are available for *similar* use. A conscious selection of one of the two methods is necessary to avoid any error that might arise from, for example, valuing the land for an alternative highest and best use and then adding the value of golf course improvements (see discussion of highest and best use, pp. 27-28).

If the appraisal assignment is such that the selection of the first method is appropriate (e.g., for sale of the golf course for homesite development), the land is appraised as if vacant and available for its highest and best use. In this case, no amount is added for golf course improvements (other than salvage value), and in fact an amount may have to be subtracted for eliminating them.

If selection of the second method is indicated (e.g., for sale of the golf course as a golf course), the only comparable sales of raw land that are valid are those whose use is recreational, open space, or agricultural, or land that is vacant and not ready for development.

After estimating land value by the second method—comparison to similar properties—the cost approach is applied. The steps in the cost approach are:

1. Estimate the current reproduction or replacement cost of the improvements.
2. Estimate accrued depreciation from all causes:
    a. Deterioration (physical wearing away of the property).
    b. Functional obsolescence (lack of desirability in utility, style, or design as compared with a property designed to serve the same function).
    c. Economic obsolescence (loss of value from environmental causes).
3. Deduct accrued depreciation to derive an indicated current value for the existing improvements.
4. Estimate the current depreciated value of accessory improvements (minor structures, parking areas, etc.).
5. Add the indicated current value of all improvements to the estimated land value to develop an indicated property value.

In applying the cost approach to a golf course, the cost of development (i.e., cost of tees, fairways, traps, greens, watering system, etc.) is added to the raw land value. The cost of replacement less depreciation of the buildings and nongolf land improvements (e.g., drives and fences) is also added. The result is a cost approach valuation of the raw land, the golf course improvements, the buildings, and the nongolf land improvements.

The value of the improvements is estimated either by a detailed quantity survey, or a unit-cost-in-place method. For the latter, the appraiser would use a cost manual in which component costs are given in various units such as square foot, cubic foot, or pound. A professional golf course architect can often furnish course improvement cost data.

An adjustment is made for depreciation of buildings and other structures as well as for land improvements such as drives, paving, and fencing. Golf course improvements do depreciate, and cost to cure should be considered in using the cost approach.[1] Natural golf course improvements, such as trees, turf, and shrubs, tend to appreciate as they mature under proper

---

1. However, the Internal Revenue Service has not allowed depreciation on greens, tees, fairways, traps, or roughs. The exception may be when the land is leased. Then the improvements can be depreciated over the life of the lease. Frequently a municipal government may lease land for a long term to a concessionaire who builds a golf facility. At the termination of the lease, which might

maintenance. However, they may deteriorate if improperly cared for, and the extent of physical deterioration represents the cost to cure.

All depreciation is estimated by personally inspecting improvements and considering age, useful life, observed condition, and utility of the component parts in comparison with similar new units.

The cost approach is most applicable in the appraisal of a new or proposed golf course of any of the three types, or in the appraisal of a private nonprofit club or municipal course where there are insufficient sales to use the market data approach or income is insufficient to use the income approach.

Two things to remember in using the cost approach of a golf course are: (1) the appraiser cannot value the land for other than golf course use and then *add* the cost of golf course improvements, and (2) unless the course is new or proposed, the value estimated will probably be value in use, not market value.

The Income Approach

The income approach is based on present value of the future benefits of property ownership. This is generally indicated by the net income a fully informed person is warranted in assuming the property will produce during its remaining useful life. After comparison of rates of return for investments of similar type and class, this net income is capitalized to an estimate of value.

The steps in the income approach, applied to golf course appraisal, are:

1. Obtain the fee schedules for the golf course being appraised and for comparable properties for the current year and for several past years. From this information, extract gross income data and trends for comparison and adjustment to develop the potential gross income expectancy.
2. Obtain and analyze use data for the subject golf course and for similar properties in the market. In the light of supply and demand trends, project a loss deduction from potential gross to derive an effective gross income projection.

---

be 20 years, the facility is turned over to the municipality. In this case the lessee might depreciate all improvements over 20 years. Normally the only depreciable items allowed by the IRS are irrigation systems, pumps, buildings, parking areas, and personal property. An irrigation system might be depreciated over 20 years, the pumping system over 10 years. Sometimes irrigation controllers are depreciated over a shorter time, such as 10 years, depending on sophistication of the system and the desires of the owner.

3. Obtain and analyze data on taxes, insurance, and other operating costs for the property being appraised and for comparable properties. Consider indicated trends and deduct a projected expense estimate from the effective gross income to derive a net income projection.
4. Estimate the remaining economic life of the improvements to establish the probable duration of income, or alternately, estimate a probable period of ownership and income stream pattern.
5. Select an appropriate capitalization method and technique.
6. Select or develop the appropriate capitalization rate reflecting the rate of return necessary to attract capital.
7. Complete the necessary computations to derive an economic value indication by the income approach.

Although the income approach is seldom appropriate in appraising a private nonprofit club or a municipal course, it is the most applicable approach for estimating the value of a daily-fee golf course because this type of facility is basically a business. Value of a daily-fee golf course is most accurately measured by application of an appropriate factor to convert earnings into value.

Again, the appraiser should remember that each golf course is a unique property, and great differences may exist even among daily-fee courses. These differences, such as physical characteristics and fee structures, greatly affect income and expenses.

For a daily-fee course, the value estimates obtained by use of the income and market data approaches will probably be close; however, for public or private courses, the income approach would probably indicate a lower value for the reasons discussed above.

RECONCILIATION OF VALUE INDICATIONS

The final step in the appraisal process is the consideration of the indicated value resulting from each of the three approaches to derive a final estimate of the defined value. Although in the appraisal of a golf course it is likely that only one of the three approaches will be applicable (based on the type of golf course being appraised), the other two approaches may also be used, even if only for a check. If all three approaches are used, the appraiser considers the relative dependability and applicability of each of the three approaches in reconciling the three value indications into a final estimate of defined value.

After examining the range between value indications, major emphasis is placed on the one that appears to produce the most reliable and applicable solution to the specific appraisal problem. The objective of the appraisal, the type of golf course, and the adequacy and relative reliability of the data processed in each of the three approaches influence the weight to be given to each approach.

THE APPRAISAL REPORT

With the final estimate of defined value, the appraiser has achieved the immediate objective of the appraisal process. As in the appraisal of all properties, the appraiser's conclusion about a golf course is then stated in a formal report for the client. This presentation of defined value is usually written and includes the data considered and analyzed, the methods used, and the reasoning followed in achieving the final estimate of value.

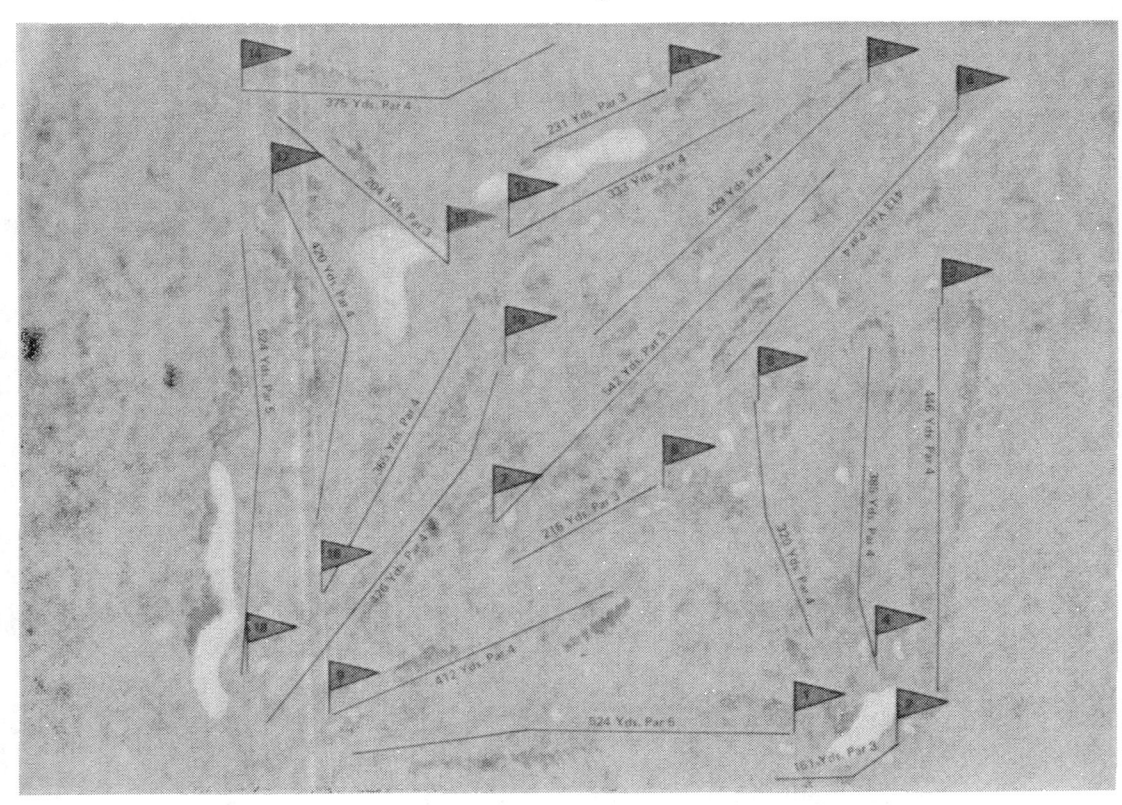

8

Valuation Under Eminent Domain

In most states the basis for valuation of property that is being taken under eminent domain is fair market value. If comparable arm's length sales are sufficient in the market, the market data approach is used to obtain an estimate of fair market value. If sales are not sufficient, the cost approach is generally relied upon for a *whole taking* and as the first of two appraisals required for a *partial taking*. The income approach usually cannot be used as a basis of valuation under eminent domain. Either the golf course is not operated as a profit-making venture; or if it is, the excess of cash flow, over and above the amount required to provide a return on the investment in land and improvements, reflects the value of the enterprise rather than the value of the property being taken. For a golf course operated as a commercial venture, use of the income approach is desirable as a check against either the market data or cost approach.

WHOLE TAKING

If the appraisal is for a taking of an entire golf course, assuming that sales are insufficient for use of the market data approach, the fair market value is the higher of the valuations found under the two methods described under the cost approach (pp. 104-106).

By the first method, the land is appraised as if vacant and available for its highest and best use. Value does not include any added amounts for golf course development or structures unless the structures could be sold separately—with an adequate sized site—for other uses.

By the second method, the underlying raw land is appraised on the basis of comparable sales available for similar use. Only sales of raw land compatible to recreational or agricultural use are considered. To the raw land value are added the cost of golf course developments and the cost of replacement less depreciation of the building and land improvements.

PARTIAL TAKING

When only a portion of the course is to be taken, a further appraisal is required. Proper procedure depends on the answers to various questions.

1. Can the course be reconstituted?
2. If not, what is its secondary highest and best use?
3. If reconstitution is possible, what is the cost to cure?

At this point a professional golf course architect is needed. The golf course architect realigns and designs the course based on land remaining after the taking plus any additional available vacant land with suitable features—that is, topography, type of soil, and water supply. The golf course architect also helps to answer other questions.

1. Will membership size be too large for the new facilities—for example, an 18-hole course reduced to 9 hole?
2. Will some of the buildings become overimprovements or obsolete?
3. Will the public or membership accept the new course arrangements?
4. Should the facilities be sold and the club moved elsewhere?

If realigning or reconstituting the course after the taking so it can still be operated economically as a golf course appears to be feasible, the "cost to cure" technique of the cost approach provides a sound basis for estimating damages resulting from the taking. Appraisal of total loss and damage under the cost to cure technique is the sum of (1) the value of the property taken, and (2) the cost of realigning the remainder into a whole golf course. If the realignment requires acquiring additional available land, the cost of additional land must be offset by the value of land taken. Obviously "double damages" could occur if both the value of land taken and the cost of new land were included in the cost to cure.

If the remaining property can no longer be used as a golf course, the basis for the "after" appraisal is provided by the fair market value of the remainder for some secondary use. This value automatically excludes everything else, except possibly salvage value of buildings and improvements that could be converted to some other use.

In some instances the appraiser must go through both procedures (a "before and after" valuation and a "cost to cure" procedure) to make sure the loss of damage estimated by the cost to cure procedure does not exceed the loss or damage estimated by the before and after procedure.

Appendix

DATA FORMS FOR THE ANALYST

To assist appraisers and other consultants in analyzing a golf course property, the following checklists and forms may be useful. The checklists enumerate items to be considered in analyses of the market, the site, and construction costs. The information forms provide for data collection on the course, the owner, course facilities and equipment, and competing courses. The forms on pages 118-123 were developed and are used by McKay Golf & Country Club Properties, Inc., Lansing, Michigan. Also shown is a list of golf course maintenance equipment bought for Arlington Lakes Golf Course during three fiscal years. It serves both as a list of equipment needed and as a representation of the cost of the equipment in the Chicago area at that time.

MARKET ANALYSIS CHECKLIST

I. Definition of trade area
    A. Location of subject course
    B. Location of competition
    C. Quality of course
    D. Quality of nearby courses
    E. Community identification
    F. Other

II. Demand factors
    A. Composition of community
        1. Income
        2. Age
    B. Climate
    C. Population growth
    D. Other recreational facilities
    E. Number of courses in area
    F. Estimated number of golfers
    G. Estimated rounds per year

III. Supply factors
    A. Number of courses in area
    B. Characteristics of courses
    C. Quality of courses
    D. Types of courses

SITE ANALYSIS CHECKLIST

I. Legal data
    A. Title and record
    B. Taxes
    C. Special assessments
    D. Restrictions and easements
    E. Legal description

II. Specific golf course site data
    A. Location
    B. Accessibility
    C. Zoning
    D. Size and shape
    E. Soil, drainage, and vegetation
    F. Water and utilities

CONSTRUCTION COST CHECKLIST

I. Golf course improvements
    A. Clearing
    B. Grading
    C. Tees
    D. Greens
    E. Fairways
    F. Roughs
    G. Hazards
    H. Watering system
    I. Cart paths and bridges
    J. Practice facilities

II. Buildings
    A. Clubhouse
    B. Maintenance
    C. Storage
    D. Other

III. Nongolf land improvements
    A. Service road
    B. Parking lots

IV. Equipment
    A. Golf course maintenance[1]
    B. Clubhouse

---

1. See list of equipment, p. 124.

(Confidential)

Course # _____
Date _____
By _____

COURSE OWNER INFORMATION

Name of golf course_____
Location_____
City_____State_____Zip_____
Name(s) of owner(s)_____
Address_____
Phone: Bus: AC _____ /_____ Res: AC _____ /_____
    Best time to call _____
Is business a corporation?_____ Partnership?_____ Proprietorship?_____
    If a corporation or partnership, have directors given authority to sell?_____
    How many are required to approve sale? _____

Are any owners or members of family working on course and not receiving compensation? _____
    How much compensation do working owners receive?_____
    Are any owners not working but receiving compensation or benefits?_____
      If so, how much?_____

Greens fee charges _____
Membership charges _____
Number of members_____Free members_____
Obligations to members _____

Obligations to adjacent property owners _____

Number of employees for golf_____Clubhouse_____
Do you have a pro?_____Greenskeeper?_____

Do you have information on three years operating income and expense?_____
Mortgages on property_____
Other courses in the area _____

Comments:

Course # _____
Date _____
By _____

GOLF COURSE INFORMATION

Name of golf course _____
Location _____
Acres in course _____ Acres in price _____
Additional land available _____
Zoning of land included _____

Number of holes _____ Yardage _____ Par _____
Course designed by _____ Built by _____
Age of course _____ Clubhouse _____ Irrigation _____
Irrigation. Greens _____ Tees _____ Fairways _____
Irrigation designed by _____ Installed by _____
Type of irrigation system: Hose _____ Quick-couple _____ Auto _____
Type of pipe _____ Water source _____
Number of wells _____ Size _____ Depth _____

Basic soil type: Sand _____ Clay _____ Peat _____
Types of grass: Greens _____ Tees _____ Fairways _____
Terrain: Rolling _____ Hilly _____ Flat _____
Woods or trees _____
Condition of greens _____ Size _____ Appearance _____
Condition of fairways _____ Size _____ Appearance _____
Condition of tees _____ Size _____ Appearance _____
Sand traps _____
Ponds _____ Lakes _____ Rivers _____
Drainage problems _____
Dikes, dams, or drains _____

Comments:

Course # _____
Date _____
By _____

CLUBHOUSE INFORMATION

Size _____ How many stories? _____ Value _____
Basement: Full _____ Walkout _____ Other _____
   Percent usable for other than utilities _____
Exterior walls: Wood _____ Brick _____ Other _____
Windows: Wood _____ Aluminum _____ Other _____
Interior walls: Plaster _____ Wood _____ Other _____
Floors: Wood _____ Carpet _____ Tile _____ Other _____
Covered porch: Size _____ Enclosed _____
Rooms:
   Lockers: Men's _____ Women's _____
   Restrooms: Men's _____ Women's _____
   Kitchen _____
   Bars _____ Liquor license _____
   Dining _____ Capacity _____
   Banquet _____ Capacity _____
   Pro shop _____
   Storage _____
   Living quarters _____
Heat _____ Air conditioning _____ Other _____
Condition of premises _____
Quality of construction _____
Design appearance _____ Suitability _____
Sewer _____ Water _____ Storm drain _____
Parking _____

Comments:

Course #_____
Date _____
By _____

OTHER BUILDINGS

Maintenance:
    Size _____
    Height sidewalls _____
    Shop area _____
    Floor surface _____
    Utilities: Heat _____ Type _____
                      Water _____ Water heater _____
                      Electricity _____ Size service _____

Golf cart storage _____

Rain shelters _____
Toilet buildings _____
Pump house _____
Swimming pool _____
Pool building _____
Tennis courts _____

Residence:
    Size _____
    Type construction _____
    Bedrooms _____
    Baths _____
    Basement _____
Garage _____
Other _____

Comments:

Course # _____
Date _____
By _____

MAJOR GOLF COURSE EQUIPMENT

Tractors _____
Trucks _____
Utility trucks _____
Trailers _____
Greens mowers _____
Fairway mowers _____
Rough mower _____
Fringe and tee mower _____
Rotary mower _____
Vertical mower _____
Other mowers _____
Spiker _____
Plugger _____
Top dresser _____
Soil shredder _____
Fertilizer spreader _____
Sprayer _____
Other _____

Pull carts _____
Golf carts _____ Gas _____ Electric _____
Rental clubs _____

DRIVING RANGE

Size _____
Direction of play _____
Location in relation to clubhouse _____
Number of tees _____
Cover _____ Heat _____ Light _____
Fencing _____
Terrain (hilly or flat) _____
Water, green, other _____
Automatic tees _____
Other _____

Comments:

AREA AND COMPETITION PROFILE

Job _____

Course Name	Dis-tance	# Holes	Pub. Priv.	Weekday 9	Weekday 18	Weekend 9	Weekend 18	Memberships Sgl	Cpl	Fam	Soc	Initn	Golf Carts Wk Day	Wk End	Comments

Land Values in Area _____

Farm acreage _____ Development land _____

Price range of housing _____

Type and condition of access roads _____

McKAY
GOLF & COUNTRY CLUB PROPERTIES

Golf Course Maintenance Equipment

Description	1977	1978	1979
Mowers			
Riding greens mowers (3)	$ 9,676.00 (2)	$ 5,321.00 (1)	—
7-Gang hydraulic fairway unit (1)	11,370.00 (1)	—	—
5-Gang pull mower fairway unit (1)	2,575.00 (1)	—	—
Riding rotary 6 ft. rough unit (1)	5,474.00 (1)	—	—
Triplex unit 84" (1)	—	—	$ 3,500.00
Hand rotary mowers (3)	500.00 (2)	250.00 (1)	—
Hand greens mowers (2)	1,400.00 (2)	—	—
Tractors and trucks			
Trucksters (2)	$ 2,697.00 (1)	$ 3,000.00 (1)	—
Mowing and utility tractor (1)	$ 7,399.00 (1)	—	—
Pickup truck, 3/4 ton (1)	$ 4,645.88 (1)	—	—
2-yd. capacity dump truck (1)	$ 6,571.80 (1)	—	—
Cultivating equipment			
Aerator (1)	—	—	$ 3,300.00
Fairway aerator (1)	—	—	$ 1,600.00
Trap rake power (1)	$ 2,571.00 (1)	—	—
Topdresser (1)	—	$ 1,700.00 (1)	—
Fertilizer spreader (fairway) (1)	$ 2,095.00 (1)	—	—
Hand cyclone spreaders (2)	—	150.00 (2)	—
Power sprayer (100-gallon truckster mounted)	—	1,734.31 (1)	—
Power sprayer (tractor-drawn, 300 gallons)	3,675.00	—	—
Power edger	—	—	350.00
Miscellaneous			
Hand blower (1)	—	—	$ 450.00
Sweeper (1) (tractor drawn)	—	—	3,200.00
Portable generator (1)	—	—	300.00
Greens thatcher attachments (set of 3) (1)	—	—	684.00
Spray hawk (hand spray gun)	$ 300.00	—	—
Backhoe for tractor	—	$ 5,495.00	—

Selected Bibliography

American Institute of Real Estate Appraisers. *The Appraisal of Real Estate,* 7th ed. Chicago: 1978.

California State Board of Equalization, Property Tax Department Assessment Standards Division. *The Appraisal of Golf Courses.* Sacramento: 1973.

Club Managers Association of America. *A Profile of the Private Club Industry.* Washington, DC: 1974.

Cole, Carlton W., "Appraisal of Golf Courses," in Edith J. Friedman, ed., *Encyclopedia of Real Estate Appraising,* 3rd ed. Englewood Cliffs, NJ: Prentice-Hall, Inc., 1978.

Cornish, Geoffrey S., and William G. Robinson. *Golf Course Design: An Introduction.* North Palm Beach, FL: National Golf Foundation, n.d.

Eckhoff, Harry C. "Daily Fee Courses: Pay-As-You-Play Country Clubs." Information Sheet DF-1. North Palm Beach, FL: National Golf Foundation, n.d.

——— "Guidelines for Planning and Building a Golf Course." *Public Works,* July 1978.

Fream, Ronald W. "Great Green Monster or Jolly Green Giant?" *Urban Land,* March 1978, pp. 5-9.

——— "How To Prevent Golf Course Maintenance Headaches." *Resort Management,* May 1978.

——— "Symbiosis: A Method of Minimizing Golf Course Maintenance Cost." *Southern Golf,* Spring 1979.

———— "Water on the Golf Course." *Western Landscaping News,* June 1978.

Harris, Kerr, Forster & Company. *Clubs in Town and Country 1978.* New York: 1979.

Herbold, Barry M. *The Valuation of Privately Owned Recreational Land.* Mimeo., n.d.

"Investing in Golf Courses." *Real Estate Investing Newsletter,* Jan. 1979.

Jones, Rees L., and Guy L. Rando. *Golf Course Developments.* Technical Bulletin 70. Washington, DC: Urban Land Institute 1974.

Milam, Robert Louis. "An Analysis of the Demand for Selected Golf Services in the North Carolina Piedmont." *The Appraisal Journal,* Oct. 1970.

Muirhead, Desmond. "Building the Golf Course," in *Land: Recreation & Leisure.* Washington, DC: Urban Land Institute, 1970.

National Club Association. *Rising Property Taxes—Can Anything Be Done?* National Club Association Reference Series. Washington, DC: 1976.

National Golf Foundation. *Golf Driving Range Manual.* North Palm Beach, FL: 1978.

———— *Golf Facilities in the United States.* 1979.

———— *Golf Operators Handbook.* 1961.

———— *The Par 3 and Executive Golf Course Planning and Operating Handbook.* 1974.

———— *Planning and Building the Golf Course.* n.d.

———— "Planning the Golf Course Maintenance Building." Information Sheet GC-27. n.d.

Norcross, Carl. *Open Space Communities in the Market Place.* Washington, DC: Urban Land Institute, 1966.

Urban Land Institute. *Land: Recreation & Leisure.* Washington, DC: 1970.

Wright, Lloyd A. *The Appraisal of Golf Courses.* Mimeo, 1967.

Data Sources

American Society of Golf Course Architects
221 N. LaSalle Street
Chicago, IL 60601

Boeckh Publications
American Appraisal Associates
525 E. Michigan Street
Milwaukee, WI 53201

Club Managers Association of America
7615 Winterberry Place
Washington, DC 20034

Golf Course Builders of America
725 15th Street, N.W.
Ste. 700
Washington, DC 20005

Golf Course Superintendents Association of America
1517 St. Andrews Drive
Lawrence, KS 66044

Golf Writers Association of America
1720 Section Road
Ste. 210
Cincinnati, OH

Harris, Kerr, Forster & Company
420 Lexington Avenue
New York, NY 10017

Marshall Valuation Service
Marshall & Swift Publication Co.
16.17 Beverly Blvd.
Los Angeles, CA 90026

Michigan Association of Public Golf Courses
15553 N. East St.
Lansing, MI 48906

National Club Association
1129 Twentieth Street, N.W.
Washington, DC 20036

National Golf Foundation
200 Castlewood Drive
North Palm Beach, FL 33408

Ohio Association of Public Golf Courses
2737 Edgerton Road
Broadview Heights, OH 44147

Oregon Golf Course Owners Association
905 N.W. Springhill Drive
Albany, Oregon 97321

Professional Golfers' Association of America
Box 12458
Lake Park, FL 33403

United States Golf Association
30 Liberty Corner Road
Far Hills, NJ 07931

Urban Land Institute
1200 18th Street, N.W.
Washington, DC 20036